A WORD of HOPE

FOR MY ABORIGINAL PEOPLE

Parry Stelter

PRACTICAL TEACHING FOR INDIGENOUS FAITH

TALL PINE PRESS
EDMONTON, ALBERTA

A WORD OF HOPE FOR MY ABORIGINAL PEOPLE

Copyright © 2014 Parry P. Stelter

Written by Parry Stelter, founder of Word of Hope Ministries, based in Edmonton, Alberta, Canada.

*If you want to use this material in any way, contact the author and give reference to this document titled: "A Word of Hope for My Aboriginal People" by Parry P. Stelter, 2014. This document may be copied in part for educational purposes, but may not be copied in whole, due to the copyright laws in place.

Unless otherwise noted, all Scriptures are from THE HOLY BIBLE, NEW INTERNATIONAL VERSION®, NIV® Copyright © 1973, 1978, 1984 by Biblica, Inc.® Used by permission. All rights reserved worldwide.

Scripture quotations marked (NKJV) are taken from the New King James Version®. Copyright © 1982 by Thomas Nelson, Inc. Used by permission. All rights reserved.

First printing May 2014
Second printing August 2014
Third printing April 2017
Fourth printing May 2020

Contact Info:

Parry Stelter, Word of Hope Ministries
Email: parry@wordofhopeministries.ca
www.wordofhopeministries.ca
Wordofhopeministries Canada

Library and Archives Canada Cataloguing in Publication

Stelter, Parry, 1968-, author

A Word of Hope for my Aboriginal People: Practical Teaching for Indigenous Faith / Parry Stelter

Canadiana 20200244221 / ISBN 978-0-98120149-7-5 (softcover)

LCSH: Indigenous peoples - Canada - Religion. / LCSH: Christianity - Canada. LCSH: Christianity and other religions - Canada. LCSH: Christianity and culture - Canada. LCSH: Indigenous peoples - Canada - Social life and customs.

LCC E98.R3 S74 2020 / DDC 270.089/97071 - dc23

CONTENTS

ABOUT THE AUTHOR........................... 5
PREFACE 7
ACKNOWLEDGMENTS........................... 9
1. WHAT A DISASTER! 11
   Introducing the Conflict 13
   A History of Deadly Approaches: Colonialism/Assimilation in the Name of God............................... 17
2. RECOVERY EFFORTS?........................ 27
   Creating a Better Understanding................ 27
   Looking at Truth 31
   A Willingness to Change...................... 36
3. THE SPIRITS ARE REAL 43
   The Foundations of Animism 43
   The Power of Animism 47
   Animism and Ceremonies...................... 52
4. CONTEXTUALIZATION & SYNCRETISM 61
   Defining Contextualization.................... 61
   Defining Syncretism......................... 63

5. **CREATION CALLS OUT** 75
   First Things First 75
   Defining General and Special Revelation. 77
   General Revelation and Missions. 80
6. **HEADING HOME** 89
   Application & Suggestions for Contextualization 89
   Final Thoughts 95
   APPENDIX 1 97
   The Flow of Destruction of the Aboriginal People. 97
   APPENDIX 2 100
   Definitions 100
   APPENDIX 3 107
   Animism is Based on Fear 107
   APPENDIX 4 108
   The Importance of the Number 4 in Aboriginal Spirituality 108
   ENDNOTES 109
   BIBLIOGRAPHY. 116

ABOUT THE AUTHOR

Parry Stelter is originally from Alexander First Nation. He and his wife Angeline are Sixties Scoop survivors. They have brought nine children into this world. Angeline has played the piano and keyboard in the church for 30 years. Parry's focus on the Bible and Angeline's focus on music make them a wonderful team. Their testimony is very powerful and is a wonderful picture of God's grace.

Parry graduated from the University of Regina with a Bachelor of Human Justice degree and from Taylor Seminary with a Master of Divinity degree. Currently he is completing a Doctor of Ministry Degree at Providence University and Seminary with a special focus on Contextual Leadership.

He founded Word of Hope Ministries, where he developed a website with a variety of free resources. He also writes columns and customized feature articles for several newspapers and magazines. Parry does pulpit supply at churches and runs workshops on anumber of issues related to the Indigenous community. He has a weekly Bible teaching program on the CIAM Media family of radio stations where the 30 minute program is played on 30 stations in Western Canada. He plans to make his project dissertation into his third book that will compliment the first two books. In the future all three books will be a rich resource for any Indigenous Christian to have, or those who work with Indigenous people.

PREFACE

It's exciting to be printing this book for the fourth time. Up until now, there are 1900 copies in use across Canada along with a handful of books in the United States. With this fourth printing, the book will be available as an e-book as well as a paperback. As this fourth printing is completed, I've finished a second book on Indigenous Christianity titled, *Indigenous People and Jesus: Making the Bible Come Alive!* The second book is a continuation of the conversation that was started in my first book, but it goes deeper into some of the issues Indigenous people face. The audience I have in mind for the second book are Indigenous Christians, and those who work with Indigenous Christian, as well as those who work with Indigenous non-Christians. In the second book I also go much deeper into my own story and show how it relates to the issues I explore.

It's my hope that through these two books and the third one that's currently being written, I'll make a connection to you the reader in a more meaningful way. The history of the Canadian and the Indigenous people is a rocky and unstable past. Colonialism has many aspects to it. The first model for Residential Schools was already being experimented on in the 1600s by the early missionaries who were zealous to convert us. Even back then, parents didn't like the idea of allowing their children to live with these strangers who wore black robes and carried a black book. There is much that has happened since that time, but certain issues are ongoing. Both books address some of those issues.

Early missionaries were persistent in using this approach to reach those who needed saving. Yet, the Gospel message is supposed to be for all people in need of a Savior. These early settlers gave the impression that Indigenous people had no idea of God and therefore they needed to be corrected. But Indigenous people had a General Revelation of God that was closer to the Gospel than we realize. It's my hope to show that there are areas of an Indigenous worldview that need to be appreciated. These two books are an intentional effort at trying to heal scars that have been engraved on Indigenous people's hearts. With these two books, and the third one that I'm working on, I want to add to the insights of Indigenous people and our traditions, by talking about the Special Revelation of Jesus more clearly, and by helping people to understand Jesus the Creator as the word of God more fully.

ACKNOWLEDGMENTS

This book could not have been completed without the support and encouragement of Dr. Allan Effa (Ray & Edith DeNeui Professor of Intercultural Studies at Taylor Seminary, Edmonton, Alberta) who proofread the initial draft document and guided me in initial research as I worked my way through a Directed Studies course as I completed a Master of Divinity Degree. I would also like to thank First Nations Alliance Church (Edmonton) for giving me the responsibility of being their Chairman of the Board, and letting me preach the Word of God on a regular basis. This helped me see my full potential as an encourager with the Word of God.

I would like to thank my wife, Angeline, who loves me and supports me in ministry and life. She was the one who encouraged me to go to seminary and fulfill my dream by working with my people.

I also need to acknowledge all the resources that are included within my bibliography, for without them I would have no research. I would also like to thank Vernon Jacob Grant (M.Div., Taylor Seminary; First Nations pastor & missionary), Dr. Willy Muller (retired pastor, missionary & professor), and Dr. Randal Rauser (Associate Professor of Historical Theology), for also completing some of the proof reading.

Finally, I would like to thank Northern Canada Mission Press (Prince Albert, SK) for assisting me in direction for the first, second and third printing of this book, and the final formatting. Tall Pine Press completed changes for the fourth printing and e-book formatting so that the book can now reach an untapped online audience around the world. Tall Pine Press is also assisting with the second book and Parry's daughter is drawing the artwork for the cover. The second book titled, *Indigenous People and Jesus: Making the Bible Come Alive!* is a must read.

CHAPTER 1

WHAT A DISASTER!

I AM ORIGINALLY FROM THE ALEXANDER FIRST NATION, BUT I WAS TAKEN FROM MY BIOLOGICAL FAMILY (BY CHILD WELFARE) AND GREW UP IN A BIBLE BELIEVING FAMILY AND CHURCH. I knew nothing of my people until I was introduced to my biological family approximately 25 years ago. My late biological mother was Cree, and my father, who I've met once (for 20 minutes), is Métis. When you look at me you will see that I am fair skinned and have a scruffy face (when I don't shave). As a result of this I could easily pass for a German man, which was the ancestry of my adopted father. In fact, when I was younger I would even tell people I was German because, when I told them I was "Indian," it changed their perspective of me in a negative way. I soon became the butt of their jokes. I do not know what it is like to be the recipient of daily racial slurs or prejudices that are addressed to my people. However, I do know that there have been terrible events that have occurred within the history of my people, and many of these events were done in the name of God.

Despite the many atrocities that have been done throughout history, many Aboriginals still claim to be Christian and fully embrace the God of the Bible. At the same time there are many who still hold true to their own beliefs and want nothing to do with Christianity. There are many Aboriginal Christians who hold differing viewpoints with regards to issues such as attending sweat-lodges, pow-wows, round dances, and praying with sweet-grass, as well as many more traditional practices. They were taught that their entire culture was not good enough for civilized people. There are liberal and conservative scholars with regards to these issues, and there is a great amount of debate going on within the Aboriginal Christian community regarding what is acceptable and what is not.

This book will assist you in making wiser decisions with regards to these vital issues that are in the midst of the Aboriginal community. This book will also enable me, as an Aboriginal man who is entering full-time ministry with my people, to make wiser and better informed decisions. The Bible will be our guide as we go on this journey together and discover the truth of Scripture and how it is applied to our lives.

First, let's define what we mean by Aboriginal. According to the Government of Canada the words "Aboriginal peoples" and "Aboriginal communities" involve a wide scope of meaning.

- **"Aboriginal peoples"** is a collective name for the original peoples of North America and their descendants. The Canadian Constitution recognizes three groups of Aboriginal people: Indians (commonly referred to as First Nations), Métis and Inuit. These are three distinct peoples with unique histories, languages, cultural practices and spiritual beliefs. More than one million people

in Canada identify themselves as an Aboriginal person, according to the 2006 Census.
- **Aboriginal communities** are located in urban, rural and remote locations across Canada. They include:
  (1) First Nations or Indian Bands, generally located on lands called reserves;
  (2) Inuit communities located in Nunavut, NWT, northern Quebec (Nunivak) and Labrador;
  (3) Métis communities; and communities of Aboriginal people (including Métis, Non-Status Indians, Inuit and First Nation individuals) in cities or towns which are not part of reserves or traditional territories (for example, the Aboriginal community in Winnipeg).[1]

As a result of the term "Aboriginal peoples" encompassing such a broad scope of people, that is why I have chosen to use "Aboriginal" as a frame of reference throughout this book, as well as the terms "Aboriginal People(s)."

INTRODUCING THE CONFLICT

The conflict that has occurred within the relationship of Aboriginal peoples and the Europeans who landed here over 400 years ago did not (only) start with the breaking of any laws, culture barriers, treaties, or any forms of colonialism. The start of the conflict that has existed for over 400 years started with the breaking of God's two greatest commandments, which are stated in His Word. We see it being stated in the Gospel of Matthew chapter 22 by Jesus Himself, but the original source comes from Deuteronomy chapter 6, when Moses was giving the people of Israel the Ten Commandments. Matthew says:

> Hearing that Jesus had silenced the Sadducees, the Pharisees got together. One of them, an expert in the law, tested him with this question: "Teacher, which is the greatest commandment in the Law?" Jesus replied: " 'Love the Lord your God with all your heart and with all your soul and with all your mind.' This is the first and greatest commandment. And the second is like it: 'Love your neighbor as yourself.' All the Law and the Prophets hang on these two commandments" (Matt. 22: 34-40).

The religious leaders of the day in biblical times were guilty of not treating the people around them with mercy, grace, understanding and forgiveness. Sixteen hundred years later the same conflicts were still alive and well.

The settlers that overtook the Aboriginal people were more focused on filling the earth and subduing it, as stated in Genesis 1:28: "God blessed them and said to them, 'Be fruitful and increase in number; fill the earth and subdue it. Rule over the fish of the sea and the birds of the air and over every living creature that moves on the ground.'" They thought this included assimilating the Aboriginal people, but obviously they were wrong. Looking back on history we know they were wrong.

When the original text was given in Deuteronomy, this command was given with even more detail and conviction:

> These are the commands, decrees and laws the LORD your God directed me to teach you to observe in the land that you are crossing the Jordan to

> possess, so that you, your children and their children after them may fear the LORD your God as long as you live by keeping all his decrees and commands that I give you, and so that you may enjoy long life. Hear, Israel, and be careful to obey so that it may go well with you and that you may increase greatly in a land flowing with milk and honey, just as the LORD, the God of your ancestors, promised you. Hear, O Israel: The LORD our God, the LORD is one. Love the LORD your God with all your heart and with all your soul and with all your strength. These commandments that I give you today are to be on your hearts. Impress them on your children. Talk about them when you sit at home and when you walk along the road, when you lie down and when you get up. Tie them as symbols on your hands and bind them on your foreheads. Write them on the doorframes of your houses and on your gates. (Deut. 6:1-9).

As Christians, our whole life and existence is supposed to reflect the grace and unconditional love that God has for us. Yet, when the Europeans came, they were so caught up in having their own way, and turning my people into proper Christians, God's greatest commandments got thrown overboard when they landed here. Dr. Allan Effa suggests that this may be as a result of the Aboriginal people being seen as "sub-human," rather than as a neighbour. This is a very insightful point that Dr. Effa makes, because the Aboriginal people were seen as sub-human and they were seen as savages. Vernon Grant says that before Confederation the Aboriginal peoples and the settlers were allies, but after Confederation it all went downhill. It started off with great potential, but it seemed to be short lived.

The rejection of God's Word and the rejection of God's grace and mercy was what started this whole problem. It seems that when we look at history, some of the European settlers taught their children (by example) to hate and to strip a people of their identity and self-worth. They did not (symbolically) tie God's law to their hands and foreheads; they used God's law to bully and subdue my people and make them feel inferior. They did not impress God's law upon their children; they impressed hatred and disregard for a people's livelihood. They did not (symbolically) write God's law on their houses or gates; they wrote laws and policies that would push the Aboriginal peoples into a cultural genocide and a vicious cycle of confusion, disillusionment and bondage. This is where the problem started, and this is what must be kept in mind when we look at the many diverse issues within this book.

Let's look closer at what didn't work in the past. Before we can move towards a brighter future we must know what went wrong in the past. Let us look to the past and see what we can discover and uncover, so that we can all learn from it and move forward in a more productive fashion.

Many people start to feel uncomfortable when you mention the residential schools and other atrocities, and they think that we shouldn't talk of these things anymore, but a true understanding can only come from first looking to that past. We must let the past become a learning tool. This chapter may be painful for some of my people, so spend some time in prayer before going any further. Ask the Holy Spirit to lead and guide you in ways that will help you move forward in a godly way. It may also be uncomfortable for some non-Aboriginal people to look at the past, because of how it reveals the negative side of our human nature. Let's all step forward together and be courageous and learn from each other.

A HISTORY OF DEADLY APPROACHES: COLONIALISM/ ASSIMILATION IN THE NAME OF GOD

Colonialism and *assimilation* are two terms that need to be defined before we can proceed to discuss what impact they have had on the Aboriginal population. *Colonialism* is defined by Merriam-Webster as follows: "The quality or state of being colonial; something characteristic of a colony; control by one power over a dependent area or people; a policy advocating or based on such control."[2] The root problem of colonialism is control, and that is what made it so terrible to its victims. Colonialism is about control over a dependent area or people. The interesting fact about colonialism is that the Aboriginal peoples were not in need of any help. John W. Friesen had this to say about the independence of the Aboriginal peoples before colonialization:

> It is becoming evident that Aboriginal Peoples of the various culture areas in North America lived full and probably satisfying lives, beginning with the fact that food was plentiful. At the time of contact, there were thriving agricultural communities around the Great Lakes Region, in the Eastern Woodlands, in the southwest, and as far north as North Dakota. Fishing was a major source of food supply on both east and west coasts, as well as among the Plateau Indians in what is now the British Columbia Interior. When the Woodland Peoples migrated to the plains several centuries ago

they developed a nomadic lifestyle following the migration patterns of the buffalo. The base of all of these cultures rested on a philosophy of ready adjustment to changes necessitated by natural forces. Many of the more sedentary civilizations left impressive remains behind which gave a clear indication of the extent of their technological genius. The eastern moundbuilders bequeathed thousands of huge temple mounds as well as burial and effigy mounds, some of which had lunar alignments. The Anasazi of the southwest left huge walled cities, some of them five stories high. Their neighbors, the Hohokam, dug hundreds of miles of water-carrying canals, many of which are still in use today. Only the Plains tribes left little physical evidence of the magnitude and genius of their cultures, save for buffalo jumps and remains of winter camps and other sites of interest to archaeologists.[3]

Many Aboriginal people had everything figured out for themselves and their survival. For some Aboriginal people, the buffalo provided everything they needed. For those that used the buffalo as a source of survival, they made use of every part of the buffalo and nothing was wasted. Their family units were already figured out and they had their own hierarchy of government. They had their own remedies for sickness and they had no need for the "white man." The "white man" was not doing any favours for these people. With favours like that, who needs enemies? The "white man" brought words such as "savage" and "uncivilized," as well as diseases, and the whiskey bottle. When we look at Friesen's description of the mound builders, we see the skill and knowledge that the Aboriginal people did possess.

Assimilation as defined by Merriam-Webster states: "The quality or state of being colonial; something characteristic of a colony; control by one power over a dependent area or people; a policy advocating or based on such control."[4] We see here that *colonialism* is linked with *assimilation* and that they are essentially the same concept. It is a matter of preference as to what word you chose to use. Throughout this book the word colonialism will be the term used to refer to this part of history.

Colonialism was used in the name of God, and that's what makes this (past) approach to living with a new people group such a hard pill to swallow. We as human beings, within the history of all humankind, have done many atrocities to each other. We must never forget that we're all equally capable of doing the most heinous crimes to one another, given the right/wrong circumstances. The people of Israel were also constantly guilty of turning away from God, despite His acts of mercy and compassion on them. In the book of Leviticus, when Moses was passing out all the laws they were to follow, he makes reference to the fact that the people used to throw their babies into the burning fire to the god of Molek: "Do not give any of your children to be sacrificed to Molek, for you must not profane the name of your God. I am the LORD" (Lev. 18:21). People have always treated each other with cruelty and ungodly practices, and that is why we must be in a constant state of self-reflection when dealing with other people, regardless of their cultural background, and avoid all ungodly approaches and practices.

Here is what Raymond Huel had to say about industrial schools, which existed within the framework of colonialism, and how they impacted the Aboriginal people:

> There is no doubt that attendance at industrial schools produced a frightening experience for

Native students as well as a sharp contrast with the world which they had known. Chief Dan Kennedy recalled that at the age of 12 he was, "lassoed, roped and taken to the Government School at Labret." Having never seen the inside of a house, he was, "thrust into a new world called civilization." He lost his tribal name and was given a new one that could be pronounced and written in English. As a further step on the road to civilization, his long braids were cut and Kennedy wondered whether his mother had died, since the cutting of hair was a sign of mourning in the Assiniboine culture. To add to the confusion, the curriculum often contradicted traditional teaching. Kennedy's "defence" was to escape three times, but each time he was captured and returned to the school. Like many other Indian children he resigned himself to becoming part of a captive audience.[5]

Both industrial schools and residential schools had a negative effect on my people, and these were an integral part of the colonialization process. I would like to know why they thought cutting someone's hair and giving them a western name had anything to do with being like Jesus Christ?

As I watched the video titled, "Muffins for Granny," a documentary on families who had experienced residential school, there was one man who told of his experience. He spoke of how the law worked on behalf of the church in keeping children in these residential schools.

> The police came out to their house on the reserve and took us kids, and because my father wouldn't

have any of this, he fought on our behalf and they had to subdue him in chains. My father was taken to prison for 6 months and when he was released he came and got us kids again and took us home. Again the police came and took us, and again my father went to prison for another 6 months. My father would arrive at the residential school, beat up the priest, and take us home. This happened over and over again. When I was there the priest would tell us that they were going to tell us about the love that the Creator had for us, but my experience was the exact opposite of that.[6]

This is an example of what colonialism (that was led by the government and the church) did to the lives of the Aboriginal people. One woman said, "I remember kids crying and the moment I was physically separated from my family, that was the worst moment of my life, and my family was never the same again. I cry just thinking about it."[7] There is absolute truth in what this woman said. This process of colonialism based on westernized Christian culture started a cultural genocide that had various negative effects.

As I watched a documentary titled, "Canary Effect," I was reminded of some of the massacres that took place in other parts of the continent, such as the United States. The United States troops were guilty of killing men, women, and children, as well as the elderly. With the help of scholars, the film looks at massacres such as Sand Creek (1864), where troops were instructed to kill and scalp everyone. In fact, Theodore Roosevelt described the massacre as being, "righteous and beneficial a decision as ever took place on the frontier."[8] There were many other facts that I discovered as I watched this film, and below is an example of why genocide was prohibited. Following that are some historical facts related to Wounded Knee, scalping, and Columbus.

- In 1948 the United Nations drafted a convention for the prevention and punishment of genocide.
- Article II. In the present Convention, genocide means any of the following acts committed to destroy, in whole or in part, a national, ethical, radical or religious group, as such:
    (a) Killing members of the group.
    (b) Causing serious bodily or mental harm to members of the group.
    (c) Deliberately inflicting on members of the group conditions of life calculated to bring about its physical destruction in whole or in part.
    (d) Imposing measures intended to prevent births with the groups;
    (e) Forcibly transferring children of the group to another group.
- Wounded Knee massacre of 1890 where U.S. Troops slaughtered 300 men, women, and children. In 1860 the entire Wiyot tribe was hacked to death as they lay sleeping. In 1853, 450 Tolowas were murdered at Yontoket. In 1854 the remaining Tolowas were exterminated. In 1850 soldiers killed the entire village of Pomo men, women and children. In 1868 General Custer killed 103 Cheyenne at Washita River (93 were old men, women, and children).
- In the 1850s the federal government reimbursed the state of California $924,259 for scalp bounties. During that decade the California Indian population was reduced by two thirds. Andrew Jackson Indian Removal Policy, en-

acted against the rule of the Supreme Court, resulted in the deaths of an estimated 25,000 Indians.
- When Columbus arrived (1492) there were an estimated 12-15 million Indigenous people in what is now the USA. In 1890 there were under 250,000 (98% gone).[9]

There are other genocides that have happened within the last 100 years, such as Rwanda and Nazi Germany, so we must never think this is the only place where genocide took place. They are happening in remote parts of the world as we speak. We must be in a constant state of self-reflection to ensure that we don't slip back into these degraded old ways. Here are four more short descriptions of what people in Residential Schools experienced as a result of colonialism, taken from the documentary titled, "Muffins for Granny":

- "When I first came to the residential school I saw a sculpture of a man who was nailed to a cross and his heart was ripped open. There was blood coming out of his wounds. When I first saw this I thought to myself, 'Is this what they are going to do to us? What did this guy do to deserve this? Who could do something like this to another person?' When you come to a place like this you don't ask these types of questions."
- "Sometimes I wonder if they had treated me a little nicer that I could have turned out to be a nicer person."
- "They used to say to us: 'We'd never turn out to be anything. We were no good. We were of the devil,' because of what we did."
- "One of my friends told me she wanted to run away, but I said, 'If you run away you'll get beaten up.' She said, 'They won't catch me.' I didn't say anything and she ran away.

The next day their bodies were found at the top of a hill just outside the school. Two men had been seen where they were caught, and when they found the bodies they were totally naked and one had been decapitated."[10]

These are (but a few) examples of what colonialism did to the Aboriginal peoples in the name of God. The Europeans thought they had a "better way" and they basically said through their actions and policies that it is, "Our way or the highway." If you don't submit we will take your land, strip you of all that is you, and place you on reservations, where you can be controlled and watched. Is it any wonder why some of my people don't trust the "white man" and Christianity? Is it any wonder why they prefer their own practices and beliefs?

Now we have to start all over again and try things differently. This is where our next section is headed. We need to ask ourselves several questions: What is the solution to this mess? Where do we go from here, knowing that millions of Aboriginal people were lost to the beliefs and actions of the "white" population? Can we recover from such a disaster? How do we understand these complex issues at hand?[11] When we truly realize the flow of destruction that was forced upon the Aboriginal people, we should fall on our knees and ask God for the strength, courage, and honor to be better people.

CHAPTER 1 STUDY QUESTIONS

(1) Do you think that the author is correct in saying that the start of this whole problem began with the breaking of God's greatest commandment (as stated in Matt. 22:34-40 and Deut. 6:1-9)?

(2) Aside from the Aboriginal people, what other people groups have been colonized? What similarities do you see?

(3) Can you forgive the people who led this cultural genocide against the Aboriginal people? If not, why not?

(4) Were you personally affected by colonialism? Are you comfortable talking about it?

(5) Is it important to talk of the past in order to move forward?

(6) Pray to God (through Jesus Christ) if you have been guilty of being prejudiced to anyone at any given time. Ask God (through Jesus Christ) to give you a heart of unconditional Christ-centred love for all people.

CHAPTER 2

RECOVERY EFFORTS?

CREATING A BETTER UNDERSTANDING

HERE ARE TWO STORIES TO HELP CONFIRM HOW WE NEED TO UNDERSTAND THE ABORIGINAL PEOPLE MORE. I was talking to an Aboriginal pastor one day and he told me a story. He said, "There was a man I knew back home and this man fasted and waited in the bush until he got a moose. When he killed the moose he took the hide from this moose, and fasted again, and made a drum. He said that because the spirit of the moose was in the drum, he was now going to use that drum to call more moose out."

I was also talking with a fellow student one day and she said that her friend is Aboriginal and attends the sweat-lodges. She asked me if there was anything demonic about participating in the sweat-lodges. I responded by saying: "This is one of the reasons why I'm writing this book, so that I can put down my thoughts (based on the Bible), along with other sources, and try to answer these types of questions."

There are some things that we have to take into consideration, when looking at these issues. Aboriginal Spirituality is based on a different worldview. This worldview embraces the use of animal spirits, and communicating with dead ancestors." She said, "My friend says when she is in the sweat-lodge she doesn't speak to demons; she speaks with angelic beings." These two stories are prime examples of what is going on in the minds of some Aboriginal people.

When you are faced with this type of mind-set, what are you going to say? It's important to talk to people in order to find out what they really believe. This is what my professors have always said: "You need to get into the mind of the person and ask them what is going on in their mind, when they talk about their spiritual experiences." The Bible says, "Satan disguises himself as an angel of light. Therefore it is not surprising if his servants also disguise themselves as servants of righteousness" (2 Cor. 11:14,15). This is something that must be kept in mind when looking at communicating with the dead and communicating with animal spirits. As Christians we are taught that the Holy Spirit is our guide and that the Holy Spirit will lead us into all truth. The Gospel of John says: "However, when He, the Spirit of truth, has come, He will guide you into all truth; for He will not speak on His own authority, but whatever He hears He will speak; and He will tell you things to come" (NKJV). If you are a Christian and you adhere to the principles of the Bible, I need to say that I don't see any Scriptures that support speaking with the dead and animal spirits for guidance.

This is where our understanding must start when evaluating where Aboriginal Spirituality fits into Christianity. We need to compare everything to Scripture, but we must also exercise our ability to love and understand first, and let that understanding start in the heart, not in the mind. It starts with what Christ has done for us. Romans chapter 12 contains a section on love. We know, as humans, that when love enters a relationship it changes everything. It changes the way we act, react and live. This is where we need to start when we look at creating a better understanding.

> Love must be sincere. Hate what is evil; cling to what is good. Be devoted to one another in brotherly love. Honor one another above yourselves. Never be lacking in zeal, but keep your spiritual fervor, serving the Lord. Be joyful in hope, patient in affliction, faithful in prayer. Share with God's people who are in need. Practice hospitality. Bless those who persecute you; bless and do not curse. Rejoice with those who rejoice; mourn with those who mourn. Live in harmony with one another. Do not be proud, but be willing to associate with people of low position. Do not be conceited. Do not repay anyone evil for evil. Be careful to do what is right in the eyes of everybody. If it is possible, as far as it depends on you, live at peace with everyone. (Rom. 12:9-18).

This passage commands us to let our love be sincere and to honor others above ourselves. It also commands us to associate with people of low position and not be conceited in the process. Ultimately, we are to live at peace with everyone. We need to get back to the Scriptures when we look at trying to understand each other. Whether someone is your enemy, or whether they are a stranger down the street, we are to treat each other with the same respect, whether we agree on matters of the Bible or not. There are many people who have preconceived ideas of my people and there are many people who are still prejudiced against "Aboriginals." We need to put aside our stereotypes and learn to love each other as the Bible commands us to. It's time to get back to the Bible when it comes to understanding the Aboriginal peoples.

The Bible gives many examples of how easy it is to fall away from God's Word and His commands. Here is a prime example from the Gospel of Mark:

> The Pharisees and some of the teachers of the law who had come from Jerusalem gathered around Jesus and saw some of his disciples eating food with hands that were "unclean," that is, unwashed. (The Pharisees and all the Jews do not eat unless they give their hands a ceremonial washing, holding to the tradition of the elders. When they come from the marketplace they do not eat unless they wash. And they observe many other traditions, such as the washing of cups, pitchers and kettles.) So the Pharisees and teachers of the law asked Jesus, "Why don't your disciples live according to the tradition of the elders instead of eating their food with 'unclean' hands?" He replied, "Isaiah was right when he prophesied about you hypocrites; as it is written: 'These people honor me with their lips, but their hearts are far from me. They worship me in vain; their teachings are but rules taught by men.' You have let go of the commands of God and are holding on to the traditions of men." And he said to them: "You have a fine way of setting aside the commands of God in order to observe your own traditions! For Moses said, 'Honor your father and

your mother,' and, 'Anyone who curses his father or mother must be put to death.' But you say that if a man says to his father or mother: 'Whatever help you might otherwise have received from me is Corban' (that is, a gift devoted to God), then you no longer let him do anything for his father or mother. Thus you nullify the word of God by your tradition that you have handed down. And you do many things like that (Mk. 7:1-13).

We, too, have been guilty of worrying about the traditions of men instead of the commands of God. Jesus said Isaiah was right when he prophesied about the hypocrites. Would Jesus be saying the same things about us (evangelical Christians) when it comes to living, accepting, and understanding the Aboriginal peoples? This is a question we all need to ask ourselves and answer, with reverence and fear before God.

LOOKING AT TRUTH

Understanding also involves entering into a dialogue with people of other religions, when trying to figure out where they are coming from, and trying to understand their own culture. Looking for truth in the Aboriginal culture is the same as looking for truth in other religions. Here is what Dean Halverson had to say about this topic:

> All religions contain some truth, and Christians should be encouraged to recognize and appreciate that truth. Islam, for example, is strong in its appreciation for the greatness of God. Zoroastrianism

emphasizes the purity of God, which demands that we too are called to be pure. Animism helps us to appreciate the truth that our battle is not just against flesh and blood (Ephesians 6:12). Taoism encourages us to be sensitive to the underlying ways of nature and to deal with the people with gentleness and understanding, not imposing our wills on them. Paul's words that God, "is not far from each one of us" (Acts 17:27) can help us appreciate Hinduism's emphasis on the immanence of God. And even atheism's hope of finding solutions through rational thinking can encourage us as Christians to be clear in our thinking and consistent in our living. While we can acknowledge, appreciate, and respect the truth that can be found in other religions, that does not mean that such religions contain saving truth that leads to salvation.[12]

The key point in all of this is that all truth can eventually lead to a saving truth. This is the bottom line of all truths. We can use these common truths to build bridges, but ultimately people need truth that will set them free. Looking for truth in other religions such as Aboriginal Spirituality creates a better understanding, and that understanding and truth will lead to a willingness to change. Dr. Randal Rauser gives insight into why those we disagree with may not be totally out to lunch with regards to knowing truth and being moral individuals. Rauser's comments were not directed towards Aboriginal people, but his advice can be made transferable to working with the Aboriginals.

In wartime it pays to keep the enemy at a distance, for it is much easier to hate and kill those we do not know. But when we come close and stare into the faces of those we are preparing to bomb, when we learn of their names and discover their passions, when we realize (as Sting sang of the Russians) that they love their children too, then our confidence in the unqualified rightness of our cause and methods begins to diminish. The same dynamic is operative in disagreement and argument. Once we come to know our intellectual opponents we can no longer dismiss them as cognitively and/or morally deficient. Indeed, we may discover that they are sometimes more intelligent and moral than we are. And here we come to an ironic conclusion that listening to our enemies just may be the best way to destroy them. "Destroy?" you reply. "A rather ironic conclusion to an irenic chapter, isn't it?" No, not the way I mean it, for as Abraham Lincoln observed, "Do I not destroy my enemies when I make them my friends?"[13]

There may be some Aboriginal people that you come across, or see in the six o'clock news, that cause you to feel like they are the enemy, but I'm here to say that the real enemy is Satan himself. The Bible says, "Be self-controlled and alert. Your enemy the devil prowls around like a roaring lion looking for someone to devour" (1 Pet. 5:8). Satan has been trying to devour my people through dominant society for years, and so we must stand up for them and be Christ to them. The Aboriginal people are not our enemies and they are not the ones to be mad at. They did not create the mess that the government legislated. They were victims of what the government did. Some people get mad because Treaty Indians don't pay taxes on the reserve and get government funding. Vernon Grant says these are but small payments for the land, gold, silver, oil, furs, and trees, that were signed away in the treaties. We must be willing to change our perceptions. We need to have a willingness to change.

There are many Aboriginal people who are very knowledgeable about life, and the way some Aboriginal people live would put some white people to shame. We need to realize that the "western way" is not the way for everyone and is not supposed to be, in the first place. This is a truth that we must be willing to look at. There are many Aboriginal people who have regular full-time jobs and take care of their homes, just like the "white man." Aboriginal people also go on holidays, attend hockey games and concerts, and take care of their houses. They take their kids to soccer, karate, and summer camp just like everyone else. Some of the Aboriginal street people give Aboriginal people (in general) a bad name, but that's because there are so many Aboriginals who are suffering in the aftermath of what was done to them in the name of God, progress and greed. When I go to homeless shelters and give my testimony, I see more non-Aboriginals than Aboriginals, which tells me homelessness and other societal issues are universal to all humankind.

Although there are many people of other religions (including Aboriginal people) that do not embrace the message of the cross, as stated in Scripture, some of these people are closer to knowing the God of the Bible than we think. Don Richardson writes on the reality of Scripture that says: "He has made everything beautiful in its time. He has also set eternity in the hearts of men; yet they cannot fathom what God has done from the beginning to end" (Ecc. 3:11). Here is what he has to say about the North American Indians and how they perceive God in their own way.

> Ask a number of Indian "lore-keepers" to describe the essence of the Sacred Four, and a consensus of their replies will run something like this: When the Great Spirit (*Wakan Tonka* to the Sioux, *Sahren-Tyee* to the Chehalis, etc.) created the world, he ordained the Sacred Four to maintain order. Thus the Sacred Four are not four gods or four demons, but four order-sustaining principles which prevent everything from collapsing in chaos.
>
> Ask Indians to articulate the Sacred Four individually and you will draw a blank. If ever Indians knew how any one differed from the other three, the knowledge has long since been lost. Indians speak of them collectively, and no other way.
>
> Is the Sacred Four concept a mere fiction? Or could it have some validity? Does the Bible hint at the existence of a God-ordained Sacred Four upholding order in the universe?
>
> I believe the answer to all these questions is yes! Consider the evidence:
> (1) The twelve tribes of Israel heading for the Promised Land always camped in four groups of three tribes each. Banners were allocated not to each of the 12 tribes, but to each of the four groupings.
> (2) Jewish altars were designed with four "horns" projecting from the four corners. Sacrifices, to be valid, had to be literally tied to all four horns, not merely laid upon an altar.

(3) The New Testament gives us four Gospels.
(4) Jesus died upon a four-armed cross.
(5) The Apocalypse speaks of four horses of four different colors, with four different riders.
(6) Finally, the Bible seems to teach implicitly that all of reality is divided into four levels of a cosmic echelon. Truly, there may be much more to the Indian concept than meets the mind at first consideration.[14]

I've often thought about some of these similarities myself, as I've come across different aspects of Aboriginal Spirituality.[15] I do believe that Aboriginal Spirituality has aspects of truth, but it's also important to realize that in order for any of those similarities to make sense, as a Christian, there must be a belief in the Gospel of Jesus Christ. At some point in time there must be an acknowledgment of what Jesus did on the cross for you, as an individual sinner who is separated from God. We cannot and should not forget to mention this, at some point in time, to those who are lost. We will get into this area more in chapter 5, when we look at general revelation and special revelation.

A WILLINGNESS TO CHANGE

A willingness to change comes from dialoguing with those who have different cultural and religious backgrounds, while trying to develop a better understanding based on common truths. Understanding these truths begins to create a willingness to change and be better stewards of God's Word, by both faith and deeds. The New Testament gives insight into the whole aspect of listening and doing, according to God's Word.

> My dear brothers and sisters, take note of this: Everyone should be quick to listen, slow to speak and slow to become angry, because human anger does not produce the righteousness that God desires. Therefore, get rid of all moral filth and the evil that is so prevalent and humbly accept the word planted in you, which can save you. Do not merely listen to the word, and so deceive yourselves. Do what it says. Anyone who listens to the word but does not do what it says is like someone who looks at his face in a mirror and, after looking at himself, goes away and immediately forgets what he looks like. But whoever looks intently into the perfect law that gives freedom, and continues in it – not forgetting what they have heard, but doing it – they will be blessed in what they do. Those who consider themselves religious and yet do not keep a tight rein on their tongues deceive themselves, and their religion is worthless. Religion that God our Father accepts as pure and faultless is this: to look after orphans and widows in their distress and to keep oneself from being polluted by the world (Jam. 1:19-26).

James says that if you get rid of all filth and evil in your life that is so prevalent, and accept God's Word that is planted in you, you will be saved. There are many of us who need to be saved from our old thought patterns, and stop pointing the finger (of disdain) at the Aboriginal people. You need to quit feeling sorry for them and encourage them; quit giving sermons and start equipping them; quit looking at them with pity and start truly loving them. Who cares if they live on the reservation and get government funding to run their band office (the government created this problem themselves)? Who cares if they have long hair? Who cares if they look different and live different (they are different)? They are human and deserve the benefit of the doubt. It isn't until we put our prejudices behind us that we will be able to create a willingness to change. Ultimately, the willingness to change comes from the heart. We need some major heart surgery – all over the world. Let's look again to God's Word for direction.

> "This is the covenant I will make with the house of Israel after that time," declares the LORD. "I will put my law in their minds and write it on their hearts. I will be their God, and they will be my people. No longer will a man teach his neighbor, or a man his brother, saying, 'Know the LORD,' because they will all know me, from the least of them to the greatest," declares the LORD. "For I will forgive their wickedness and will remember their sins no more" (Jer. 31:33-34).

> Get rid of all bitterness, rage and anger, brawling and slander, along with every form of malice. Be kind and compassionate to one another, forgiving each other, just as in Christ God forgave you. Be imitators of God, therefore, as dearly loved children and live a life of love, just as Christ loved us and gave himself up for us as a fragrant offering and sacrifice to God (Eph. 4:31-5:2).

God's Word is consistent from the beginning of the Old Testament right through to the end of the New Testament. It gives us words that will comfort us, convict us of our sins, lead us into truth, and show us the way we should go. Although this book includes many opinions and stories of others, the main references for our problems are within God's Word. This is where we need to start and end. This is where we need to start when we look at developing a heart which has a willingness to change. It starts by getting on bended knee and saying, "I'm sorry, God, for all my preconceived perceptions of the Aboriginal people, and please give me a willingness to change, regardless of my current views and opinions." If you are an Aboriginal person, you may also want to pray for a heart of forgiveness, and ask God to help you as you continue to move on.

CHAPTER 2 STUDY QUESTIONS

(1) What are some misconceptions that non-Aboriginal people have about Aboriginal people?

(2) What are some traditions (of the western way) that have hindered the Aboriginal people from becoming what God wants them to be?

(3) What are some elements of truth that the Aboriginal people have? Remember that not all truths are "saving" truths, but looking at these areas of truth will be helpful in creating a better understanding.

(4) When looking at Don Richardson's "Sacred Four" concept, what other aspects of the Aboriginal culture reflect a concept of God or biblical ways of thinking?

(5) Pray that you will be willing to find aspects of truth in other religions (especially Aboriginal Spirituality) that can be used to create a better understanding of where people are coming from. Pray that you can use those truths to point all people (especially Aboriginal people) to Jesus Christ and their need of a Saviour).

(6) If you have never accepted Christ as your personal Lord and Saviour, would you be willing to do that now? God knows how we think. That is more important than the

words we use when we pray. If you are unsure of what to say to God, you can invite Jesus into your life through a prayer like this: "Lord Jesus Christ, I know I am separated from God because of being born with a sinful nature. I now admit that I am a sinner in need of a Saviour. Forgive me for all my sins and make me the person You want me to be. Thank You that You will not use any of my past sins against me. Thank You that I now have a secured place in the kingdom of God in this life and the one to come. Thank You in Jesus' name. Amen."

CHAPTER 3

THE SPIRITS ARE REAL

The Foundations of Animism

Let's take a look at what animism means and then we'll delve into talking about the power of animism, and what that looks like within some ceremonies. According to Worldview Resource Group, here is a definition of animism:

> *Animism:* a worldview that understands human existence to be environed by numerous and diverse spirit beings and impersonal forces that affect human experience and well-being. It is held within this system that man can control or significantly influence these capricious entities by proper incantations, rituals, offerings, sacrifices, or magic to bring about desired outcomes. Animistic man's regular pursuit is to stay in control of all aspects of life, with all things serving his will.[16]

Animism is a complex set of beliefs that have everything to do with worldview. The way a person views the world is how they are going to interpret the everyday things that happen in their lives, whether they be positive or negative. Animism is directly linked to the spirit realm and is an integral part of the power struggle within the spirit world. It is much the same as a Christian's belief in the spiritual realm, but from a different worldview. Animism is part of many world religions and is not exclusive to the Aboriginal people. It is our job as Christians to show them that, although the spiritual realm is real, God is ultimately still in control of everything that happens. The future does not depend on harmonizing with the spirit realm (outside of what Scripture teaches), but relying on the finished work of the cross. Here is what Sydney Page had to say about the spirit realm:

> In the New Testament, the story of Jesus is told against the backdrop of the demonic. One of the important motifs running through the story is conflict, and not just conflict between Jesus and human opponents. All of the Evangelists portray Jesus as being in conflict with Satan and demons. In seeking to entice Jesus into disobedience, the devil exhibits cunning not unlike that of the serpent in Genesis 3. In his efforts to lure Jesus into putting God to the test, Satan even cites Scripture. But despite his evil intentions, Satan is subject to divine control. The temptation originates as a result of the Spirit's leading, is completely unsuccessful, and culminates with Satan's departure.[17]

This is what we need to teach and show the Aboriginal people. Yes, there is a spiritual realm but, because of what Jesus Christ did for us on the cross, we are set free and we have full access to God through Jesus Christ. We don't have to live in fear[18] and we don't have to allow Satan to scare us into thinking he's in control. Satan's power is real, but God's power is stronger and God is ultimately in control of everything, including Satan, demons, or spirits.

Now we will take a look at what Denise Hodgman had to say about what animists believe. Hodgman presents 24 markers of an animistic worldview. Hodgman states that the list is not exhaustive, but portrays a "detailed picture." Here is a breakdown of the 24 markers:

(1) Animists believe in personal spirits.
(2) Animists believe in impersonal spiritual forces.
(3) Animists believe that the spirit realm causes events in the human world and natural world.
(4) Animists believe that the spirit realm can at times be hostile.
(5) Animists seek to find out which spirit or spiritual force has caused which event.
(6) Animists seek to determine which spirits will cause which event in the future.
(7) Animists live in fear and need security.
(8) Animists seek spiritual protection.
(9) Animists believe humans can control or manipulate these spirits/forces.
(10) Animists believe all aspects of reality to be interconnected.
(11) Animists are human-centred rather than God-centred.

(12) Animists are focused on the present rather than the eternal.
(13) Animists are more concerned with power than with truth.
(14) Animists tend to be highly relational people.
(15) Animists are more concerned with social sin than theological sin.
(16) Animists give a great deal of attention to death.
(17) Animists assign significance to dreams.
(18) Animists have a concept of a distant and benevolent high god.
(19) Animists favor orality.
(20) Animists focus on the local rather than the universal.
(21) Animists believe in an impersonal cosmic order.
(22) Animists believe that a person can be vulnerable to attack of evil spirits by proximity.
(23) Animists believe that a person can be vulnerable to attack of evil curses by curses.
(24) Animists consider healing and sickness to be spiritual issues.[19]

This list gives many insights into the worldview of believers in animism. When you take a closer look at the worldview of the Aboriginal people, you begin to realize that there are reasons for everything they do and say. Not every Aboriginal person will adhere to this worldview, but this list gives a good description of where large portions of my people are coming from.

Our job, as Christians, is to help them transform their worldview from one of power and fear, to a worldview that sees Jesus Christ as the one who sets us free from the bondage of fear and the power of the enemy. Satan loves to keep my people in the bondage of fear, and have them reject the work of the cross. They need to be shown that when Moses brought the people of Israel out of the bondage of slavery in Egypt, that this biblical event was a forerunner to Christ bringing the entire human race out of the bondage of sin from Satan. Keeping this in mind, let's take a closer look at a more detailed description of the power of animism within the Aboriginal context.

The Power of Animism

Animism does have a power behind it. Unfortunately, that power is not the same power that comes from trusting in the Lord Jesus Christ. Mary Dean Atwood compiled a guide for tapping into the spiritual realm, based on Native American Spirituality. She gleans her work from many people who are seen as teachers in this area. In one of the chapters of her book, she has a section titled, "Choosing Your Animal." Within this section you will find a detailed guide on how to tap into the spirit realm and find your power animal. Remember that animists believe in power and control and that everything in nature is connected. This section should help you realize what powers are being tapped into, as part of the worldview of some animists.

> *Option One:* Keep requesting your power animal to appear until it does. It will have to appear several times to indicate its dedication to you. You cannot choose an insect, or any fish, reptile, or animal with fangs or bared teeth. After finding your power animal (no dialogue is necessary), you may bring the animal out with you or leave it in the Lowerworld. The latter is recommended for your first power animal retrieval.

Option Two: This method is recommended for those experienced in achieving imagery or trance states or those who already have done a power animal retrieval. (The dialogue is easier to handle and less likely to influence or interfere with your vision.)

Soon you will see animals around you. If you do not see any, ask your power animal to appear. Be firm in repeating your request that your animal may reveal itself to you. If the animal is on your left side, walk on by. If it comes up behind you, walk away. The only animals that can come from those directions are creatures such as gophers or snakes. If the animal is in front of you or on your right side, it may be your ally. It must have either black, shiny eyes, gold, sparkling eyes, or red eyes. Red eyes are indicative of older primeval allies. Any other color will be unsatisfactory.

You should ask the animal three questions:
(1) What is your name?
(2) Will you obey every instruction I give you?
(3) How will you help me improve myself?[20]

It became clear to me, as I read this guide to entering into the spirit realm to obtain an animal spirit, that this does not fit within the parameters of Scripture. I should mention that there are many Aboriginals, who are traditional, that would not approve of Attwood writing this book and giving such advice. They would adhere to an Elder or medicine man/woman giving them an oral teaching in the traditional way. Yet, at the same time, the procedure of obtaining an animal spirit may look similar in nature. Traditional Elders teach that you are not to use any of these powers for evil but, with any kind of power, the temptation to abuse it is always there. The issue that I want to make is not what they do with the power of attaining spirit guides, but the fact that animists are looking for power outside the parameters of Scripture, and anything outside of the parameters of Scripture is not of God, no matter how good it is packaged.

Winfried Corduan looks at *Nature Spirits*.

> Though most traditional religions recognize the triad of god, nature spirits, and ancestor spirits, they tend to attach varying importance to each. Most Native American religions grant the highest recognition to nature spirits. The world for them is made up of living personal spirits, not inanimate matter. Each plant, animal, unusual rock or body of water may be sacred because there is a spirit in it. Many cultures promote the practice of informing a deer, for example, of its impending fate before killing it in a hunt. This custom is frequently interpreted in terms of maintaining harmony with the natural world, but fear of retribution from the spirit of the animal is no doubt relevant as well.[21]

Notice how the author describes, "Native American religions granting the highest recognition to nature spirits."[22] This is why you see so much importance with the significance of animals such as the Eagle, the Wolf, the Bear, the Owl, etc. They all have meanings for the different tribes and groups of Aboriginal people. Each tribe has specific animals that have a special meaning for them and that meaning is rooted in the spirit world of animism. Each individual may also have an animal spirit that has a special meaning for them as well. One thing to keep in mind is that not all Aboriginal people believe or practice these animistic beliefs. We must be careful not to classify all Aboriginals in the same category.

I came across another interesting book that describes a man who was once a "witch doctor" and how he came to know the Lord Jesus Christ. His book shows the darker side of animism, from his own experience. The book tells many stories of his journey out in the bush, thus the title, "The Bushman and the Spirits," by Barney Lacendre as he told it to Owen Salway. One of the chapters is titled, "I Sought the Spirits," and so I give you some insight into this man's life and how he confirms the power involved in animism.

> Mary Beade's father was a witch doctor; one of the best in the north. Mary was the mother of Hazel and Freddie. I have seen her father, Frank Beaverskin, put rattlers of a rattlesnake in his hand, sing, and watch the rattlers as they made a noise. Frank's hand would be perfectly still, but the rattlers would shake.
>
> I became very interested in witchcraft as I watched him work as a witch doctor and as I listened to the stories he would tell me.
>
> Witchcraft had been part of my life since I was a child of five or six. I remember how an old witch doctor used to come to my stepfather's ranch. It's like a picture in my mind's eye, seeing the old man of about 75 years jumping down from his wagon and shaking hands with my stepfather and mother. Sometimes he'd camp right in our yard and stay a few days.

> In time he showed us a shirt he was wearing when he was fighting the Blackfoot Indians. He was an idol worshipper and worshipped many kinds of spirits. He invited them into his life and gave himself over to the devil. Among the spirits he worshipped was the spirit of stone.
>
> He had given himself so completely over to the spirit of the stone that bullets could not penetrate his body. His shirt was full of bullet holes, but the bullets would drop off as they hit his body.
>
> Now, all I can do is tell you these things. Whether or not you believe them is up to you. Many of these things concerning witchcraft I have seen with my own eyes. I am now a Christian and I am telling you only what I believe in my heart.[23]

It is up to you whether you believe his story or not, but the Bible does makes it clear that Satan's power is real. As Christians we have the assurance that Satan's power is limited in the life of a believer. He can make our lives uncomfortable at times, but we have the ultimate victory, based on what Jesus has done for us, through the work of rising from the dead. This is what we need to focus on when dealing with Aboriginal people who have these animistic beliefs. We need to show them that the power of Jesus Christ is much more powerful and influential than any spirit that comes from nature.

Mary Pat Fisher and Lea W. Bailey give more insight into how my people view nature, and how that view is tied with the spirits. "We must try and worship the land, the ground and the stars and the skies, for they are the ones that have spirit. They are the mighty spirits which guide and direct us, which help us to survive."[24]

According to what I've been taught about the Bible, the Holy Spirit – who Jesus left as a deposit on the guarantee to come – is the only Spirit that we are to want to guide us and help us survive. The Aboriginal people must be shown that the Holy Spirit is the only reliable Spirit to have for guidance and survival, because the Holy Spirit comes directly from God the Father (Creator of the Universe), and not from an animal spirit, or any other kind of guide.

The New Testament is full of examples of the power of Satan. I give you a passage from the Gospel of Luke that describes this: "He (Jesus) replied, 'I saw Satan fall like lightning from heaven. I have given you authority to trample on snakes and scorpions and to overcome all the power of the enemy; nothing will harm you. However, do not rejoice that the spirits submit to you, but rejoice that your names are written in heaven'" (Lk. 10:18-20). Aboriginal people do not have to fear any nature spirits; they only have to believe on the Lord Jesus Christ and transform their worldview from a belief in animism to a belief in Jesus Christ. Our next section is a continuation of the power of animism, through ceremonies, because ceremonies and power are linked together.

ANIMISM AND CEREMONIES

The uses of ceremonies within the Aboriginal community are coming into the open and making a comeback within the Aboriginal community. There are a variety of ceremonies that do exist, but we will not take the time to discover all of them. Some of the common ones known are the sweat-lodge ceremony, the round-dance ceremony, and the pow-wow ceremony. There are many more, but a more in-depth look at these would require further research. For our purposes we will look at the Pow-wow and the Sundance (not necessarily in that order).

The documentary titled, "Spirit Doctors," highlights medicine men and women who told their story of how they've helped their people with their teachings.[25] In the film it was stated that through the language of the Native people, they are connected to their culture, their ceremonies, the earth and spirit world. It also stated that, "For nearly 70 years the Indian Act outlawed our sweat-lodges, pot-latches and sundances. These ceremonies were at the very heart of our very existence." During the filming of the project one of the technicians discovered that he had cancer, which he said was hard to accept. With both of his parents passing away from cancer, it affected him profoundly. He says, "It forced me to re-examine what my role really was in this world."

Being a believer in western medicine, he changed his mindset and started to look to the traditional ways to tackle his battle with cancer. During the filming of this documentary, he sought healing through a traditional way of healing. He became part of a ceremony seeking healing from the Creator through the use of ancestral and animal spirits.[26]

Seeking healing from God is what we are supposed to do, if we are a believer in Jesus Christ, and if we believe that the Bible is our guide book for life. We have to be aware of these approaches when seeking healing. Do we adhere to stories of healing from those with animistic beliefs? We know that there is power in animism but, as believers in Christ, we are to seek healing directly from God. This is what we need to impress upon believers in animism. Jesus Christ brings true healing: spiritually, emotionally, physically, and emotionally. We don't seek healing from the created things in nature; we seek healing from the Creator of all things.

Is the Pow-wow that my people embrace any different from someone who is involved in square dancing, jazz dancing, ballroom dancing, or simply dancing at a wedding? This is something that needs to be looked at. I've heard many stories from fellow non-Aboriginal Christians who say they remember going to pow-wows as a kid and watching the "Indians" dance. It was something they did every summer.

Do we as Christians need to be cautious about attending pow-wows? If you are an Aboriginal Christian, do you go to pow-wows? If you are an Aboriginal Christian, do you participate in pow-wows as a dancer? These are questions that I've had for years and, even though I've attended an Aboriginal church for over 10 years, I've never heard of these questions being answered objectively. They are never talked about from the pulpit, and it's because everyone is afraid to bring it up for fear of opening old wounds, or offending someone. Occasionally I've heard stories of how certain family members are very superstitious, and of encounters with medicine men, and the dark side of those encounters, but I've never heard of these questions being talked about out loud. If I would have heard of these concerns being talked about, I would have no need for this book. Occasionally I've had conversations with people in private and, as soon as I bring up the subject of these questions, they immediately have an opinion.

I can see some of the psychological and physical benefits that pow-wow dancing can have on the dancers, because many people will say that it makes them feel alive and that it improves their self-esteem. I get that and I understand that, but there is more to the dancing than just feeling good. The dancers say that when they dance they are entering the spirit world and are becoming one with the web of nature. This is where it starts to cross the line and goes against what the Gospel of

Jesus Christ teaches. If I were not a Christian and someone told me that pow-wow dancing improved their self-esteem I would say, "Great! Fantastic! Do it whenever you can, as much as you can." But I am a Christian and when someone says that, when they dance, they are entering the spirit world and that the regalia (outfits) they are wearing carries the spirits of the animals, I become cautious and say, "This is entering into the animistic spirit realm now and I'm starting to feel uncomfortable." The dancers are dancing to the "Creator," but are using animal spirits as a mediator to bring their praises to the "Creator."

On the surface, pow-wow dancing seems innocent, but be aware of what you are getting yourself into, if the pow-wow is not focused on Jesus. You are joining these people in their celebration of entering into the spirit world. Most of the dances represent a connection with the Creator through animal spirits. The outfits are beautiful and it takes the dancers years to fine tune their outfits, and their dance moves, but the end result is that many attempt to reach God through a spirit world that has nothing to do with Jesus Christ and the work of the cross. The question that has risen within other circles has been: can these ceremonies/dances be redeemed through contextualizing them? My response is: everything must be measured against Scripture and that is the bottom line for any group that is considering adopting these practices. If you are a Christian and you pow-wow dance, my question is: are you worshipping God through Jesus Christ? If you are ... great! If you are not, then maybe it's time to re-evaluate your motives. There are people who dance for fun and know nothing of this spirit connection, but it's still important to point out that many dancers do believe in the animal spirits helping them to dance. Once again there is no blanket answer to all of this. My daughters, who are being raised by their kokum, dance in the pow-wow, but they are just having fun. Yet, sooner or later they need to understand why some of the dancers do what they do and have it all aligned with Scripture.

The Sundance is another ceremony that is still practiced today, and in the past has often been associated with pain and suffering through the piercing of skin. Mary Pat Fisher gives us insight into the Sundance and what the dancers experience when they are involved in this ceremony:

> The suffering which each dancer willingly undergoes is heightened during piercing ... at some point during the dance, incisions are made in the skin of their chest, back, or arms and sharpened sticks are inserted.
>
> Why must the dance involve so much suffering? A Lakota sun dancer explains, "Nobody knows why, but suffering makes our prayers more sincere. The sundance tests your sincerity, pushes your spirit beyond its limits."[27]

For those Aboriginal people who still practice these ceremonies, it is our job to inform them that Christ paid the penalty of suffering and the debt is already paid. There is no need for further suffering, except to suffer for Christ when persecuted. I should add that the person that was interviewed did not even know why he was suffering so much. He just thought that suffering made his prayer more sincere. This is how serious many Aboriginal people are with regards to ceremonies. The sacrifice they make is often more of a sacrifice than any of us Christians make. Even though their suffering may seem misdirected, it still says a lot about the character and integrity of my people.

We can learn from this and try to be more sincere in our commitments to God.

Christopher Partridge had this to say about why there is a resurgence of ceremonies amongst the Aboriginal people: "The disregard for the earth, for community, for spirituality, have brought the whole human enterprise into jeopardy. Arising like the phoenix from the ashes, tribal peoples are gathering again in their ceremonial circles, remembering discarded teachings, renewing the traditional ways."[28]

We can't really blame the Aboriginal people for wanting their ceremonies back, for in their experience, the religion that was presented to them (in history) obviously does not live up to their words. It is still our job, as Christians, to show them a saving truth within the worldview of our faith in Jesus Christ.

Kay Johnston described the experiences of people who dance in the pow-wows, and shares what is going through their minds as they go through this process. She interviewed several people and each of those interviewed gives their own subjective interpretation of what is involved in pow-wow dancing. You can see the animistic beliefs come out in their statements:

> Dancing the Grand Entry[29] for me is one of the best parts of the pow-wow, whether it's an inter-tribal or competition pow-wow, because to me it represents one of the spiritual parts of the pow-wow. The way I was told is: when they dance in the flags and the colors, they're bringing in the spirits of the ones who have gone before us and they are dancing there with us, like we are taking part in something old and something sacred ... They say when you're dancing, that the spirit – that's the one that guides you when you dance – will take over you and the

way you dance. And that's what makes you feel so good when you dance ... I think of the eagles and the hawks, the swans. The spirits of those birds live on in the feathers that we wear. They carry us and help us to be light, and our spirits to be light. They say that because the eagle flies the highest, it carries our thoughts and our prayers to the Creator.[30]

When a non-Christian is dancing in a pow-wow, they might be guided by the spirit of an animal, so caution and wisdom may be necessary. If you are a Christian and you are going to have a pow-wow, it should be focused on Jesus Christ in order to be more biblical. When I look at Scripture, I know that I am covered by the blood of Jesus Christ, and the finished work of the cross, and so if I attend a non-Christian pow-wow to visit family and friends, I have nothing to fear.

David J. Wishart gives further insight into the Sun Dance Ceremony: "The Sun Dance is a distinctive ceremony that is central to the religious identity of the Indigenous peoples of the Great Plains."[31] This gives evidence to the fact that ceremonies, in general, are an integral part of the worldview of the Aboriginal peoples. The Sun Dance Ceremony is an integral part of the worldview of some of the Aboriginal people of Canada. "The ceremony is highly variable because its performance is intimately connected to the authoritative guidance of visions or dreams that establish an individual relationship between one or more of the central participants and one or more spirit persons."[32] This ceremony is linked with trying to access the spirit world through visions, dreams, and a variety of spirits.

Paul Hiebert gives great advice to Christians and shows how they should respond to adherents of other world religions, especially on how to help them transform their worldviews:

> Christians must move beyond immediate ministries to the long and difficult task of transforming people's animistic worldviews into biblical ones. If we simply work within traditional explanation systems, there is a real danger that the Gospel will be transformed into Christo-paganism-animism with a Christian veneer. New Christians often see Christian prayers as magic formulas, Bible verses as amulets, and preachers as magicians more powerful than their old ones. Christianity is perceived as powerful witchcraft and spiritism, but the fear of witchcraft and spirits remains. People's ideas about well-being, misfortune, and evil must be transformed by biblical teaching as much as their understanding of the nature of God.[33]

There is a great need for people who are willing to live with an Aboriginal people group and teach them the fundamentals of the Bible. Whenever you come across an Aboriginal (in your church), it will take time and patience, not because they are difficult people, but because many have a worldview that is ingrained into every aspect of their lives. This is more prevalent for those who were raised in their own Aboriginal communities, especially if they were raised by their grandparents, or if they experienced the residential school environment. We, as Christians, need to show them that we love them and, if they keep their focus on Christ and the Scriptures, that there are many aspects of their culture that they can keep. Godly wisdom must always follow with respect to crossing any spiritual lines. I think it is wrong to outright condemn these ceremonies, but if you are a Christian you need to know these things. Then you can make your own decision and that will be between you and God to decide.

CHAPTER 3 STUDY QUESTIONS

(1) Do you agree with the definition of animism as described in this chapter?

(2) What are some examples of people living in fear within the animistic worldview?

(3) What are some Scriptural references that describe the spiritual battle that we are in?

(4) When looking at Denise Hodgman's paper, "24 markers of animism," what do you agree with and disagree with?

(5) What examples from Scripture can you come up with that describe animistic beliefs?

(6) Pray that God (through Jesus Christ) will give you wisdom and discernment about which spiritual forces are of God and the Word of God, and which are not. Pray that you would realize that Satan's power is real and nothing to be messed with, but that God (through Jesus Christ) has all power, authority and dominion in this life and the one to come. Pray that the blood of Jesus Christ would protect you and your family from all spiritual forces, because Jesus Christ is our Passover Lamb that saves us from the power of death and fear.

CHAPTER 4

CONTEXTUALIZATION & SYNCRETISM

Defining Contextualization

THIS CHAPTER IS ON CONTEXTUALIZATION AND SYNCRETISM. At first I was going to have two separate chapters – one on the former and one on the latter – but I soon realized that the two concepts are often taught together and you can't talk about one without talking about the other. We will start off by looking at where the development of contextualization came from, and how it is defined. According to Daniel Shaw, this is what contextualization is all about:

> Contextualization is an extension of the old "indigenous" concept. It came into vogue in the late 1970s and has been the subject of many articles in journals such as *Missiology* and numerous books in recent years (Gilliland 1989, Hesselgrave 1989). It

is no accident that contextualization theory and worldview theory have developed side by side. This growing literature focuses on the need to take the local culture and its worldview seriously, and use the concepts vital to a people's daily living to present the Gospel. In this way the Gospel has relevance within the context of presentation. Therefore the nature of the Gospel and the church that develops within a cultural context will vary.

One of the problems facing new Christians, and the missionaries among them, is how they should handle their old beliefs and rituals. Several approaches have been tried, resulting in variations of meaningful understanding of the Gospel in a cultural context. These variations range from syncretism to a viable church.[34]

It seems that contextualization has come about as a result of the church and mission organizations realizing their mistakes. They realized the methods that they've used in the past, with regards to reaching the unreached areas of the world (for Jesus Christ), have not worked as well as they had hoped they would. Contextualization came as a reaction to new believers not being grounded in their faith, or unbelievers responding with little conviction or concern for the Gospel of Jesus Christ. When missionaries, pastors, and lay people saw practices outside of Scripture taking the place of a well grounded faith in God's Word and Jesus Christ being the foundation of faith, they realized something had to be done.

DEFINING SYNCRETISM

When I say syncretism I mean, "An individual or certain people group becomes a Christian(s), but still hang onto some of the aspects of their traditional religion, that are not honouring to God's Word." Yet, according to Peter Schineller, syncretism can have different meanings to different people.

> Both in the history of its usage and in contemporary usage, "syncretism" has had varied meanings. Originally it was applied to political alliances in ancient Greece. Some Old Testament scholars use it to describe the process by which ancient Israel assimilated elements from surrounding cultures. In the age of the Reformation it pointed to the links between Christianity and humanism; and also to the need for Protestant and Catholic churches to come together. Today it retains many of these meanings, with both positive and negative connotation. As used by anthropologists and historians of religion, it may be used either positively or negatively. Whether one takes a positive or negative view will depend on how one defines syncretism, and usually will reflect a conservative or liberal stance.[35]

This is usually what I have witnessed, as I've come across the different points of view of how Aboriginal Spirituality should be used in the Aboriginal Church. I've come across both conservative and liberal views. Let's start with the conservative view. Bill Jackson, who has written a fair amount of literature and has experience as a missionary and pastor with Aboriginal people across Canada, had this to say about syncretism:

> The dictionary definition: "A combination of varying and often opposed beliefs, principles or practices, especially those of various religions." The Scripture in 2 Corinthians 6:17-18 is very clear that the Lord God wants us, the believers, for Himself. "Therefore, 'Come out from among them and be separate ... and I will receive you.' I will be a Father to you." This fellowship and worship is centred on Jesus Christ. We are to have no part of that which we participated in while in the old life. It's not just another religion we got into since we got saved; it is salvation through a living person – Jesus Christ. "Come out from among them" does not mean that the believer leaves and goes on to live elsewhere, but "come out from" participating in a worship or practice where Jesus Christ does not have the pre-eminence.[36]

Jackson is very strong in his belief about syncretism, but I know his perspective is based on the Word of God and his personal experiences with his people. This is why there is so much conflict that goes on with regards to adopting old practices, or not adopting old practices. It's a sensitive subject that is being addressed on an ongoing basis. Hopefully, this book will help you with that process. Jackson also says that people (in general) should not be involved in ceremonies such as the sweat-lodge. "Since there is communication with spirits in the sweat-lodge, Christians should not be involved. Even though some may be classed as good spirits, God has not given us any direction to initiate any contact or communication with angelic beings."[37]

Now we look at an individual who holds a more liberal view of contextualization. Richard Twiss, a Sicangu Lakota (now deceased), was part of a movement that endorses the use of traditional practices, as long as they do not conflict with Scripture. There are many aspects of Aboriginal Spirituality that are not spoken of directly in Scripture, but the Word of God is still to be used as a measuring stick, as much as possible, in any context. Twiss had this to say about contextualization and what is happening with the Aboriginal people:

> Many Native pastors and leaders are praying in a traditional way, burning sage, cedar or sweet-grass as part of their prayers. Others are meeting in a traditional sweat-lodge ceremony as a place of worship, intercession and accountability. Others are praying with a "pipe" ceremony and holding rites of passage ceremonies for their sons and daughters as a place of discipleship. Others are using traditional designs, cultural religious motifs, musical styles, ceremonies, rituals, symbols and indigenous names and languages as vital components of their contextualization efforts.[38]

There are a lot of questions that people have when you look at these different approaches to contextualization. I can also see where Twiss is coming from, because of the issues surrounding the colonialization period, and his work with his people, but these are issues that have been coming to the surface more and more and they are not going away. I don't have all the answers to these dilemmas, but I do know that we have to use discernment and the Scriptures as our sounding board when deciding whether to adopt either approach.

Paul Hiebert has done a fair amount of work in this area and he shows four methods of contextualization that were developed by Jacob Loewen. I will show you a breakdown of those four methods:

> *Exegesis of the Culture:* The first step in critical contextualization is to study the local culture phenomenologically. Here the local church leaders and the missionary lead the congregation in uncritically gathering and analyzing the traditional beliefs and customs associated with some questions at hand. For example, in asking how Christians should bury their dead, the people begin by analyzing their traditional rites: first by describing each song, dance, recitation, and rite that makes up their old ceremony; and then by discussing its meaning and function within the overall ritual. The purpose here is to understand the old ways, not to judge them.
>
> *Exegesis of the Scripture and the Hermeneutical Bridge:* In the second step, the pastor or missionary leads the church in a study of the Scriptures, related to the question at hand.
>
> *Critical response:* The third step is for the people corporately to evaluate critically their own past customs in the light of their new biblical understandings, and to make decisions regarding their response to their new-found truths. The Gospel is not simply information to be communicated. It is a message to which people must respond.
>
> *New Contextualized Practices:* Having led the people to analyze their old customs in the light of bib-

lical teaching, the pastor or missionary must help them to arrange the practices they have chosen into a new ritual that expresses the Christian meaning of the event. Such a ritual will be Christian, for it explicitly seeks to express biblical teaching. It will also be contextual, for the church has created it, using forms the people understand within their own culture.[39]

Creating a dialogue with the Aboriginal people you are working with is essential in developing a method of contextualization with them. When someone from an Aboriginal community has a relative who dies, the burial (funeral) process is quite different, especially if the wake and funeral ceremony takes place in the Métis Settlement, First Nation community, or village.

Here is my subjective experience at traditional wakes in the Aboriginal community. It is traditional for there to be a wake, as soon as the body is released from the funeral home. This usually takes place over the course of 1-3 days. The body is put in a casket and sits in the corner of the living room, if it's in a house, or at the front of the room, if it's in a community hall or recreation centre. There is usually a fire outside that stays lit for the entire event, while family and friends come and go. The family of the deceased offer food and beverages, as well as plenty of chairs to sit on. If it is in a house the entire living room is cleared out for the body and the rest of the space (in the living room) is reserved for chairs that go around the outside walls of the room. An Elder usually sits beside the body giving prayers for the deceased and family, while burning sweet-grass or sage.

When the wake is over they have a feast that has many rules to it. They then take the body to the cemetery and do another short ceremony, just before the body is buried. It's not uncommon for the men to grab a shovel and put all the dirt back into the ground, until it is all done. This ritual of death has many components to it, and I only gave a brief description of it from my past experiences. I never mentioned what the fire is for, or the details of the feast, or views on the afterlife. You may have to do some research of your own, but this is a great starting point. This is why it is so important to sit down and talk with an Aboriginal person and find out what they believe in and why. Different tribes have different beliefs and practices. There is no "one size fits all" mentality to the spiritual and cultural beliefs and practices of the Aboriginal People.

Victoria Freeman describes what she has discovered within her studies of the Aboriginal people in Canada.

> Not surprisingly, a contentious issue is the resurgence of traditional spiritual practices. Reverend Davidson spent two years at the United Church's Francis Sandy Centre for Aboriginal Ministry before coming to Sarnia in 1996; there she gained an appreciation for the traditional spiritual teachings and practices of Aboriginal people. She has tried to incorporate some elements of traditional spirituality into her ministry, and is convinced that much can be synthesized with Christianity. "There is a need for us to explore beyond the literal teachings of Christianity to the spiritual, and there we will find our Native heritage," she wrote to me, and added diplomatically, "Many are willing to take this journey, while others remain firm in the teachings of the first missionaries." In fact, some members of the congregation have left St. Clair United, and

gone elsewhere for Christian services that do not incorporate Native teachings.[40]

What Freeman explains here is exactly what is going on in the Aboriginal community. There are Aboriginal people all across North America who have adopted different methods of making the Gospel more relevant to them. Some groups can be classified as being successful in contextualizing their congregations, and feel at peace with what they're doing. There are others who are seen as syncretising the Gospel, but yet they feel at peace with what they've done. It's like a Baptist trying to convince a Pentecostal to stop speaking in tongues, or a Pentecostal trying to convince a Baptist to try being baptized in the Holy Spirit. It's never going to happen. I feel that these groups of people will probably not come into agreement with each other, and so it is important to make a decision on your own based on Scripture, godly counsel, and investigation of your own with the discernment of the Holy Spirit. The liberal camp and the conservative camp will always be in disagreement with each other and usually with highly emotional feelings.

I read an interesting book titled, "Whiteman's Gospel," authored by Craig Smith, a Chippewa Indian from Leech Lake Reservation in Minnesota. He says something very profound as he talks about, "Christianity and Today's Indian." Smith doesn't use the word contextualization, but you can read between the lines and discover what he's talking about:

> Not too long ago, denominational leadership from one denomination came out with a paper on "New Methodologies on Reaching Native Americans." When Native leaders made inquiry as to who developed this paper, and who was included in their

research, they found out, much to their dismay, but not to their surprise, that this entire document was compiled without any Native person's involvement. It was written exclusively by Anglo leadership, and the people they contacted in their research for this document were all non-Indian leaders of other denominations and mission organizations. Not one single Native person was interviewed, nor were any Native person's views included in a powerful document that was going to provide the new and "more effective" philosophy of ministry that this denomination was to engage in as it worked among Native Americans! No wonder why Native people continue to feel that the Gospel is the "Whiteman's Gospel!" Can we really blame them?[41]

I think it's safe to say that Smith has a point. Contextualization does not occur in a vacuum, behind closed doors. It occurs in a dialogue that happens between all interested parties, such as the leadership and the congregation. They work together with patience, love, and acceptance, in one hand, and with Scripture in the other.

Craig Ott had this to say on contextualization and syncretism:

> What are the limits of appropriate contextualization, and how can we protect the process of contextualization from the danger of syncretism? Syncretism is, "the replacement or dilution of the essential truths of the Gospel through the incorporation of non-Christian elements" (Moreau 2000b, 924). Some modern scholars are not concerned

about syncretism, suggesting that it is a natural, neutral blending of ideas between religions that takes place all the time. "Since all churches are culture based, every church is syncretistic," they purport (Moreau 2000b, 924; see also Schineller 1992). However, this ignores the biblical emphasis on God's absolute truth, which is the foundation and the measure of all interaction with culture. Both the Old Testament (e.g., Deut. 12:4; Judg. 2:19; 2 Kings 17:16-17) and the New Testament (e.g., 1 Cor. 8-10, see above; Col. 2:8-23, see Arnold 1996) clearly warn God's people against their natural tendency to blend their beliefs and practices with those of the dominant culture in ways that stray outside God-revealed truth and God-acceptable practice.[42]

This author seems to have a good grasp on what contextualization is and what syncretism is, therefore it is with this type of perspective that we can approach contextualization. We must see God's Word for what it is and realize that we are accountable to God, not to those around us. As you reach out to Aboriginal people, you must keep in mind that issues of contextualization and syncretism are paramount to understanding the best way to present the Gospel of Jesus Christ, and maintain the Gospel of Jesus Christ for generations to come.

Terry Muck had this to say about contextualization:

> Deepening relationships with those of another religion and culture opens the door to discovering the metaphors that might be most apt for communicating the Gospel. God goes before us into another culture. God's wisdom can be found in many as-

pects of another religion. Those points of contact can become the links that lead a person or a community to find the pearl of great price, to embrace the Gospel, and to find life in Christ.[43]

Muck makes a great point. We need to try and help the Aboriginal people find the pearl of great price, so that they can embrace the Gospel of Jesus Christ, and find life in Christ. There are so many Aboriginal people who are suffering in silence and need a Saviour, and they need a friend who will accept them for who they are. They need to see the accepting eyes of Jesus in you. They need to feel the love of Jesus in your presence. They need to experience the joy of Jesus in your laughter, and they need to experience the healing power of Jesus in your friendship. It's up to you. You can be the one to lead them closer to the Lord. You can be the one who shows them the Jesus who they've never known. You can be the one who lives the example of Jesus out in your life, in real time, with real people. You can be the hands of Jesus and bring healing with the oil of gladness and joy.

CHAPTER 4 STUDY QUESTIONS

(1) Do you agree with the term "contextualization," as described in this chapter? Why or why not?

(2) Do you agree with the term "syncretism," as described in this chapter? Why or why not?

(3) What examples in Scripture point to the use of contextualization?

(4) Do you agree with Richard Twiss and his view of contextualization? Why or why not?

(5) What are some ideas that you have had with regards to making the Gospel more real to the Aboriginal people?

(6) What conflicts have you encountered as people have tried to adapt old ways in making the Gospel come alive? Why did these conflicts occur?

(7) Pray for wisdom and discernment when applying any traditional practices passed down to us from our ancestors. Pray that you will measure everything against Scripture, the power of the Holy Spirit, and Godly counsel.

CHAPTER 5

CREATION CALLS OUT

First Things First

The purpose of this chapter is to show that Aboriginal Spirituality, as a case study, is an example for how people of other religions have a general revelation of God. It is important to point out that I am not stating that all people have a special revelation of God, through Jesus Christ, but they do, in fact, have a general revelation of God.

Scripture is where we need to start when we, as Christians, are looking at how God reveals Himself to people of other religions. We do not have to agree with all of their practices, but we do have to acknowledge that they do have a starting point from which to work with, and that God is fully aware that this is where they are at. It is our job, as Christians, to share the Gospel of Jesus Christ with these people and let God use what is already in place (a general revelation of God), and move them closer to a saving knowledge of Jesus Christ (a special revelation).

Taking a closer look at how my people, and people of other religions, have this general revelation of God will be the focal point of our discussion. Firstly, we will look at how we define having a general revelation and special revelation of God; secondly, we will take a look at how people of other religions have access to this general revelation of God; and thirdly, we will look at some specific examples of how people, within the Aboriginal context, also have access to this general revelation of God.

When Christians speak of God, we are speaking of the Triune God, who consists of the Father, the Son, and the Holy Spirit. The three persons of the Trinity are fully explained in the Apostles' Creed. We will not go into the different views of the Trinity, or the history of the Apostles' Creed itself, but we will simply use the Apostles' Creed as a description of who God is according to the Scriptures. Understanding the Trinity and the Apostles' Creed is not an easy task, but we will use it to start out, because of its vital importance to this discussion.

> *The Apostles' Creed:* I believe in God the Father almighty, maker of heaven and earth; and in Jesus Christ his only Son our Lord, who was conceived by the Holy Spirit, born of the Virgin Mary, suffered under Pontius Pilate, was crucified, dead, and buried: he descended into hell; the third day he rose again from the dead; he ascended into heaven, and sitteth on the right hand of God the Father almighty; from thence he shall come to judge the quick and the dead. I believe in the Holy Spirit; the holy catholic church; the communion of saints; the forgiveness of sins; the resurrection of the body, and the life everlasting.[44]

This creed is part of the foundation of our faith, as Christians. Next, I will define what I mean when I refer to the terms general revelation and special revelation of God.

DEFINING GENERAL AND SPECIAL REVELATION

The term general revelation of God, as described in the *Evangelical Dictionary of Theology*, is:

> The divine disclosure to all persons at all times and in all places by which humans come to know that God is, and what he is like. While not imparting truths necessary for salvation – such as the Trinity, the incarnation, or the atonement – general revelation conveys the conviction that God exists and that he is transcendent, immanent, self-sufficient, eternal, powerful, good, and a hater of evil.[45]

I will not go into a word study of these different words – such as: the meaning of the Trinity, incarnation, or atonement; or into a study of the attributes of God – such as: transcendent, immanent, self-sufficient, eternal, powerful, good; or about God being a hater of evil. What I will do now is define the term "special revelation," and then we will continue on how a "general revelation" of God is evident in the lives of many Aboriginal people, as well as people of other religions.

The term special revelation, as described in the *Evangelical Dictionary of Theology*, is:

> Special revelation is redemptive revelation. It publishes the good tidings that the holy and merciful

God promises salvation as a divine gift to humanity which cannot save itself (Old Testament) and that he has now fulfilled that promise in the gift of his Son in whom all people are called to believe (New Testament). The Gospel is news that the incarnate Logos has borne the sins of the doomed, has died in their stead, and has risen for their justification. This is the fixed center of special redemptive revelation.[46]

Does God reveal Himself to all people, even if they have never heard about Him, or even if they do not believe in Him, as described in the Apostles' Creed and the Bible? We will continue our discussion by searching the Scriptures, as stated in the book of Romans: "For since the creation of the world God's invisible qualities – his eternal power and divine nature – have been clearly seen, being understood from what has been made, so that men are without excuse" (Rom. 1:20).

This is the starting point for our discussion. As I looked at some of the commentaries on Romans, I discovered some insight that describes what the Apostle Paul said within this passage. The *Holman New Testament Commentary* says:

> Paul will demonstrate in this section of his letter to the church at Rome that people with perfectly good insight have looked all around the world and never seen what is plainly evident – the signs pointing to the existence of God. Creation boldly declares the glory of God, as the psalmist puts it (Ps.19:1), through what God has made – and yet the natural human tendency is to look at the evi-

dence and suppress it, offering the excuse that he never saw it at all.[47]

Paul says that, "Creation boldly declares the glory of God." This is also what we will discover when we look at the work of Arnold F. Fruchtenbaum, who argues that a general revelation of God refers to how, "God reveals himself to all men."[48] He goes on to say that, "General revelation is to supply man's need for spiritual answers and to persuade the souls of men to seek after God."[49]

God reveals Himself to all of humanity, and the sole purpose is to draw all people to Him. When I look at the way that the oceans, the seas, the lakes, and the rivers are all interconnected, I can't help but be in awe that there is a divine presence that created it all. When I look at the four seasons that occur on a regular basis here in Canada, and other parts of the world, I can't help be amazed at how these four seasons keep the cycle of life going in perfect harmony. When I look at the perplexity of the human body and how it preserves itself and functions, I can't help but think that there is a divine designer behind it. When I look at the beauty and greatness of the galaxies, I can't help but see that God was the one who put them all in place, and continues to keep them in place. When I see the complex nature of the animal kingdom, including all the different types of insects, bugs, and organisms, I find it hard to deny that God is the one who created and sustains all of it. Yet without a special revelation of God through Jesus Christ, this general revelation of God (by itself), just condemns those who don't believe in Jesus Christ, because God says that because of this general revelation they are now without excuse.

GENERAL REVELATION AND MISSIONS

Let's continue to discover how God reveals Himself to people of other religions. Timothy Tennent will be our guide for the next portion of our discussion, due to his expertise in theology and missions. Tennent states in one of his books that, due to globalization, we must, "Engage with ideologies of unbelief and with Non-Christian Religions."[50] He states that when we take a closer look at how the Gospel has grown and flourished in Africa, it doesn't take long to see that God was not seen as a deity that was imported from Europe, but rather as a God who was already there, "although known and worshipped only dimly and needing the full revelation of the person and the work of Christ as revealed in Scripture."[51] Tennent then goes on to say that there are a number of theological reflections of this when we look at it in today's context. He says that when we look at doing missions work with other world religions, it is important to know that we need a greater knowledge of their sacred texts, so that we can see glimpses of this general revelation of God within their texts, and see something in common with them, instead of opposing that culture. Other world religions already have a general understanding of who God is, we just have to keep leading them toward a saving truth in Jesus Christ.

Don Richardson wrote a popular book where he describes his experiences of being a missionary to the Sawi tribe in New Guinea. His stories and theological reflections, as a missiologist, are still alive today. In *Peace Child*, Richardson finds a unique way to share the Gospel of Jesus Christ with this cannibalistic tribe. The tribes were fighting against each other, but decided to bring peace within this tribal community, and the way they did this was offer a peace child. Each tribe offered a child to the other, and as long as each child remained alive there would be peace between the two tribes. Richardson saw a way that he could share the Gospel message to these tribes in a way that they could understand it. He said that God offered His son to the world as payment for our sins and this is God's peace child to us. It is payment for the price of peace. We will now take a look at one reaction to Richardson's theological point of view on general revelation.

Bruce A. Demarest and Richard J. Harper reflect on Richardson's arguments for general revelation and redemptive analogies within the books, *Peace Child* and *Eternity in Their Hearts*, which we shall look at shortly. Richardson refers to the fact that many people who have not heard the Gospel are closer to God than we think, and he uses several examples to prove these redemptive analogies that exist in the Bible and from his personal experiences with tribal peoples. Demarest and Harpel agree that Richardson has done some good work, but they argue the validity of some of those claims.[52]

When we look at Richardson's *Eternity in Their Hearts*, we see him describing, from a number of different cultural perspectives, how people around the world already have a general revelation of God. He combines biblical narrative with the cultural beliefs of a vast array of people groups to prove this, and he asks the reader an important question. That question is this:

> *Question:* If God gave two pagan peoples – Canaanites and Greeks – prior witness of His existence, could He not also have extended the same or at least a similar providence to other pagan peoples as well? Perhaps even to all of them? In other words, has the God who prepared the Gospel for all peoples also prepared all peoples for the Gospel? If He has, then the current assumption, held by

millions of believers and non-believers alike, that pagan people cannot understand and generally do not want to receive the Christian Gospel, and that it is therefore unfair (and almost more work than it is worth) to try to get them to accept it, must be a false assumption.[53]

Here is that response to Don Richardson:

> In his book, *Eternity in Their Hearts*, Richardson relates theologically the concept of redemptive analogies to God's self-revelation. Richardson believes that the redemptive analogies he covered in world cultures occupy an integral place in God's scheme of making Himself known to all persons everywhere ... Christians concerned with world evangelization must applaud Richardson's zeal to bring the Gospel to unreached peoples. His soul-winning efforts reflect the heart of a dedicated pioneer missionary. But the present writers have certain misgivings about Richardson's concept of redemptive analogies and the way he relates these alleged intimations of the Gospel to God's self-revelation ... It is also important to realize that in its universal disclosure, general revelation performs the limited function of enabling all persons to know that God is and something of what He is like ... Romans 3:10-12 supports the judgment that general revelation does not provide saving knowledge of God.[54]

The article goes to say that, although general revelation does not save, it does serve three functions. These are:

(1) A sense of metaphysical dependence on God;
(2) A sense of moral accountability to God;
(3) A sense of the need for acceptance by God.

What I appreciate about looking at these two different perspectives, is that you still come to the conclusion that a general revelation of God does, in fact, exist; and that it is a starting point in which to work with, when dealing with people of other religions and sharing the Gospel. It is interesting to see that a general revelation of God with people of other religions does exist. I agree with Richardson that God has given people of other religions a prior witness to the Gospel and that these people will be open to you sharing the Gospel with them because of this starting point.

I would like to add to this discussion the words of Dan Story and show you his biblical perspective of how God will respond to those who have acknowledged a general revelation of Himself, but not necessarily a special revelation through Jesus Christ. He refers to Romans 1:18-25, where God reveals Himself through nature. Story says that this is the best example of God revealing Himself through nature, and that God sees the unbeliever as someone without excuse. He goes on to say that if these non-believers do not respond to God through general revelation, that their fate is far worse than the ones who had accepted God's general revelation, yet both will be guilty of rejecting God by not accepting a special revelation of God through Jesus Christ.[55] The fate of those who do not believe in a special revelation in Jesus Christ is eternal separation from God, and so discussing the different levels where this may occur may be futile, because when you are separated from the presence of God, it not something that you would want to wish upon anybody. No matter which way you look at it, it is an eternal separation from God, which is to not be desired, or wished upon anyone.

According to Stanley E. Porter, he says that there are many inclusivist theologians out there and they come in many different colors. These include a variety of theologians including Clark Pinnock and Gerald Dermott. Porter and Cross state that Pinnock's inclusivist view comes out of his book titled, *A Wideness in God's Mercy*, and that one of his main points is that God offers "a universal means for salvation, rather than a restricted means."[56] They also state that Pinnock does not see all world religions as positive, but sees the work of the Holy Spirit within a large portion of them. Pinnock says that, "Because of cosmic or general revelation, anyone can find God anywhere, at any time, because he has made himself and his revelation accessible to them. This is the reason we find a degree of truth and goodness in other religions."[57]

I would wholeheartedly agree with Pinnock on the fact that other religions do possess elements of truth and goodness, but any truth or goodness has to be eventually fulfilled in the work of Jesus Christ. I do believe that Richardson and Pinnock are correct with regards to other religions having a general revelation of God. One common denominator that all of these sources have agreed upon is that it is possible to have a general revelation of God, regardless of your religious and cultural background. Ultimately, we all need a special revelation through Jesus Christ in order to be saved. Now we shall turn to the issue of general revelation within the Aboriginal context.

As someone who is of Aboriginal origin, and who has family members who practice Aboriginal Spirituality, there is one common thread that is woven throughout my observations of the life of an Aboriginal person. That one common agreement is that we are a people that believe in the spiritual realm and, within this belief system, there is a powerful reverence for there being a Creator. The animistic beliefs of some of my people who do not believe in Jesus Christ are grounded in the workings of the spirit world, where dead ancestors and animal spirits play an integral role. Ultimately they do refer to God as Creator and to them this general revelation of God is accomplished through nature. Some of my people have a worldview where everything is connected through nature and, when one part of that cycle is broken, it affects all the other parts. This same concept can be seen within Scripture when the Church is seen as the body of Christ.

> The body is a unit, though it is made up of many parts; and though all its parts are many, they form one body. So it is with Christ. For we were all baptized by one Spirit into one body, whether Jews or Greeks, slave or free, and we were all given the one Spirit to drink. Now the body is not made up of one part but of many. If the foot should say, "Because I am not a hand, I do not belong to the body," it would not for that reason cease to be part of the body. And if the ear should say, "Because I am not an eye, I do not belong to the body," it would not for that reason cease to be part of the body. If the whole body were an eye, where would the sense of hearing be? If the whole body were an ear, where would the sense of smell be? But in fact God has arranged the parts in the body, every one of them, just as he wanted them to be. If they were all one part, where would the body be? As it is, there are many parts, but one body. The eye cannot say to the hand, "I don't need you!" And the head cannot say to the feet, "I don't need you!" (1 Cor. 12:12-21).

This passage goes on to say more about spiritual gifts but, for the sake of our discussion, this will give us a good basis for seeing how everything is connected. When we look at this passage in an Aboriginal context, the body of Christ is seen as one unit. Within an Aboriginal context we also see humanity and nature working as one unit, but there needs to be an emphasis on the person of Jesus Christ, in order for this to be eternally meaningful.

The *Journal of North American Institute for Theological Studies* had an article titled, "Missional Community," and it gave some good insight into the Aboriginal people having a general revelation of God. There were several examples given in this article, but the example I will use comes from the worldview of the Nuu-chah-nulth (an Aboriginal people group of British Columbia). We, as Christians, are told from Scripture that whatever we do, to do it for the glory of God. The Nuu-chah-nulth people are prime examples of this being lived out in real time within their own community. What they believe and practice is a direct reflection of possessing a general revelation of God.

> Spirituality is not tacked on to the programs we offer; it is central and persistent through all aspects. Caring for young people, working in the kitchen, picking up garbage, or driving a boat are spiritual acts as much as drumming, singing, or Bible studies are. We are reminded of the words of Paul: "Whatever you do, do all to the glory of God" (1 Cor. 10:31). In this worldview all of life is intertwined between the physical and the spiritual. Hunting, fishing, government issues, justice issues, family life are all both physical and spiritual activities. All

physical realities were birthed in the spiritual. The Nuu-chah-nulth thus have a clear understanding of the transcendence of the Creator.[58]

This Aboriginal group has a general revelation of God and it is an integral part of their lives. This is where a group such as this puts some of us as Christians to shame. God reveals Himself through nature and when you learn lessons from nature, such as harmony, it is directly applicable to our lives and the way we are supposed to live. These people see everything they do as an act of respect to God, and this has to be acknowledged as a general revelation of God.

When the Europeans came to this continent, many of the Aboriginal people already had a general revelation of God, and all they needed was some encouragement to seek a special revelation through Jesus Christ. Despite these mistakes of the past, we must realize that it's not too late. My people have not given up on themselves because, more than ever, they are fighting for their rights. We, as Christians, can tell people of other religions as well as the Aboriginal people, that we acknowledge that they already have a general revelation of God. This same God also desires them to have a special revelation through Jesus Christ to make that revelation complete. This is the challenge that is before the Christian community but, as long as we have air in our lungs, we have to keep working with all people. Everyone has been given a general revelation of God, and God wants Christians everywhere to honor that when sharing the special revelation of God through Jesus Christ to people of other religions. God wants Christians everywhere to realize that He uses nature, among many other aspects of Himself, to reveal who He is. As a result of God's general revelation, we are all without excuse as to the existence of God.

CHAPTER 5 STUDY QUESTIONS

(1) How often does your church recite the Apostles' Creed? Should we do it more frequently? Expand why.

(2) Are there Scriptures that define our faith, that have similar aspects of the Apostles' Creed?

(3) Do you believe that people can have a general revelation of God? Why or why not?

(4) Do you believe that every human being is without excuse with regards to the existence of God? Why or why not? Give specific examples.

(5) Is it fair that all people will be judged at the end of time, even if they have never heard the Gospel? Why or why not?

(6) Pray that you will be able to acknowledge the general revelation which God has used in revealing Himself to followers of other religions. Pray that you will be able to take that general revelation and point people to a (saving) special revelation through Jesus Christ.

CHAPTER 6

HEADING HOME

APPLICATION & SUGGESTIONS FOR CONTEXTUALIZATION

EVERYTHING WITHIN ABORIGINAL SPIRITUALITY IS CONNECTED TO THE SPIRIT WORLD, WHICH INCLUDES DEAD ANCESTORS, NATURE, ANIMALS, AND ESSENTIALLY ALL OF CREATION. To someone who is traditional in their ways, they will hold a worldview that is tied to this type of thinking. I turn to an example of the Yup'ik Eskimos to prove my reasons for this. Keep in mind that whether you are dealing with Yup'ik Eskimos, Plains Cree, Blackfoot, Blood, Cheyenne, Hopi, Haiti, Stoney, Ojibwa, Cherokee, Sioux, or the Navajo, you are dealing with a similar worldview. They may look different in some of their practices, but they all are similar in nature. Most believe in a Supreme Being or Creator of the Universe, but that Supreme Being is not always rooted in Scripture, or the person of Jesus Christ. Here is what the Yup'ik do as they prepare for winter:

> After freeze-up in November, Yup'ik Eskimos gathered in their winter villages, where they enjoyed a number of public celebrations that marked winter as the ceremonial season. Five major ceremonies were performed during this period, three of which focused on the creative reformation of the relationship between the human community and the spirit world on which they relied. In all three ceremonies (the Bladder Festival, the Feast for the Dead, and the masked dances known as Agayuyarag) members of the spirit world were invited into the community, formally hosted, and finally sent back out of the human domain. This ritual movement effectively re-created the relationship between the human and spirit worlds and placed each in the proper position to begin the year again.[59]

The Yup'ik's worldview is engrained in the spirit world, and so is the worldview of those Aboriginal peoples who hold onto animistic beliefs. Yet not all Aboriginal people are animists. There are some who adhere to a variety of beliefs. There are Catholic Aboriginals, Protestant Aboriginals, and Animistic Aboriginals, and there are those who believe in a bit of everything, but you won't find many Aboriginals who are atheists, because most believe in God as the Creator. Enter into a dialogue with them and ask questions, rather than assume you know what they believe.

I would like to give you some insight into how contextualization happened in the life of an Aboriginal Christian. There is a book titled, *The Council Speaks: Answers to Questions Native North Americans are Asking*, and within this book are questions and answers to a variety of intriguing questions that were asked from Aboriginal people. In the chapter on, "Culture and Religion," there is an explanation on "Sanctification of Indian Religion" written by Adrian Jacobs. This book is a compilation of questions and answers that have appeared in the "Indian Life" newspaper column over the years. Jacobs says that every culture has positives and negatives, but there is no need to throw every aspect of your culture out. This is what he says:

> I have retained some Indian values as they are in line with the Word of God. For example:
> (1) Respect for Elders – every "good" Native knows and practices this.
> (2) Care of the Earth – Adam was told to "tend" or "guard" or "keep" the Garden of Eden. I never littered before I became a Christian and I don't now.
> (3) Importance of Extended Family.
> (4) Awareness of the Spirit World.
> (5) Thanksgiving to God for all His blessings.
>
> There are many other things that are not a violation of the Word of God, and therefore do not need to be abandoned ... Sanctification requires thinking and the application of the Word of God to our lives. It may be scary to let Native Christians grow up and judge their own culture in the light of God's Word, but it is what God desires. "Religion" does all your thinking for you. God wants you to grow up and judge all things in the light of His Word.[60]

This is what I've been trying to solidify throughout this book. Everything has to be measured against Scripture and, even if some people are making mistakes, we have to let them find that out for themselves, as they look for God's direction. All of this requires patience, understanding, love, and a willingness to change. We have to look back to the past and see where the problem started, which includes a history of mistakes instituted by colonialism, and make better decisions in the future. We have to create a better understanding of the Aboriginal people and have a willingness to change. We also have to try to understand animistic beliefs and how they are intrinsically tied with a certain worldview, while at the same time realize that the power within animism is real, and that ceremonies are a vital part of Aboriginal life.

When we've done that, we can develop methods of contextualization, while keeping in mind the dangers of syncretism. This is a long process that takes a lifetime, but we all have exactly that. We all have a lifetime to serve God and present the Gospel of Jesus Christ in a clear and concise manner to those who do not see it as clear and concise. My people are different, but aren't we all? The Aboriginal people have experienced tragedy and loss, but haven't we all? Let's reach out and help the Aboriginal people find an answer to all of life's questions, and help change the problem that was created over 400 years ago.

There are aspects of Aboriginal culture that you can incorporate into your sermons, as a minister of the Gospel, such as the use of legends and proverbs within the Aboriginal context. R. L. Gowan compiled a short booklet titled, *Legends of the Trail: Inspiration from Indian Stories, Proverbs and Psalms*. It is within a booklet like this that you can find great treasures of contextualization without watering down the Gospel through syncretism. Here is an example of one story that will open your eyes to the possibilities that are out there and that you can create:

Death Sickness

Once long ago a dreadful disease spread through the Umpqua tribe. Many people died. Few who had the disease lived. Hundreds of people, both young and old, slept their last sleep. Day and night the death chant was heard in the teepees. At last the medicine man decided what to do. "We will climb to the top of the Big Mountains. There we will be closer to the Great Spirit and he will hear our cries." The people took down their teepees and followed the medicine men. The climb was long and hard. At last they camped in a meadow on the mountains. But the sickness followed them.

Then Teola, the chief's daughter, became ill. The people loved her and grieved for her. They called her the Little Mother of the Umpqua. She was tall and straight as an arrow and as graceful as the willow tree. One dark night they thought death had come for Teola. Around the fire in front of her teepee the men sat with their heads bowed. Inside her teepee the women marched around her mat and chanted the death song. Then a strange thing happened.

A deer, white as snow, stepped out of the dark forest. Unafraid, it walked across the meadow to Teola's teepee and circled it three times. Silent, wondering, the men watched it enter the teepee. Teola stretched out her hand to it. The deer came close, touched her lips, and then walked off into the night. As soon as the deer had gone, Teola rose and called to her people, "I am well! The angel of the Great White Spirit has kissed away my sickness."

> Christ Jesus was like the white deer in the story. What He did is not a legend – it is true. God's Word tells us about it. One day sin came into the world. Since then all men everywhere have sinned. With sin came death. Before that none died. Now all men do (Rom. 5:12). But God, the Great Spirit, loved His people. He did not want them to die. He wanted them to live forever with Him. Then he sent His Son, His only Son Jesus, into the world. Many times Christ touched people who were ill and made them well. But His real purpose for coming was to heal them from the sickness of sin. To do this He had to die on the cross for them. He not only died, He rose again. Now those who are sorry for their sins can be forgiven. When they die, they can go to live forever with Him.[61]

This is contextualization that is measured against Scripture. It states within the story that this is a legend and that the Bible is not a legend. It separates truth from fiction and leaves the person with thoughts of what Jesus has done for them, not what things within nature have done for them. You can use this within an evangelistic message and people will relate to it, and see the Gospel of Jesus Christ for what it is. It starts with a legend and ends with Scripture. This is what it is all about.

Final Thoughts

Throughout the course of this book we've looked at where the whole problem of colonialism came from, and the problems associated with it. We've looked at creating a better understanding, looking at truth, and a willingness to change. We've had a closer look into animistic beliefs and worldview. We then delved into contextualization and syncretism and how these two terms have to be understood together. We then looked at how the Aboriginal people do have a general revelation of God, but ultimately need a special revelation of God.

We have just skimmed the surface with regards to these complex issues and this book is in no way comprehensive or complete. This document has been a mere guide to growth and change. God can restore my people, and He can change the hearts of both the Aboriginal people and the non-Aboriginal people. We can do our best to contextualize the Gospel of Jesus Christ within the Aboriginal Christian community and watch out for syncretism, but the Holy Spirit will be the one that will truly change people's hearts. The Holy Spirit is the one who leads and guides us into all truth. It is my prayer that you read this book with one hand and use the other hand to hold the Word of God. The change that needs to occur starts with one person at a time. Step forward and be one of those individuals.

CHAPTER 6 STUDY QUESTIONS

(1) What are some of the approaches that your church has tried with success?

(2) What are some of the approaches that your church has tried without success? What are some of the conflicts that occurred? What can you do to avoid these conflicts in the future?

(3) If you are an Aboriginal person, have you felt uneasy in a non-Aboriginal church? Why or why not?

(4) If you are not an Aboriginal person, have you been guilty of making Aboriginal people feel uncomfortable in your church setting? If not, how have you made an effort to make them more comfortable?

(5) Pray that God (through Jesus Christ) will guide you by His Word and by the power of the Holy Spirit to empower the Aboriginal people around you to be proud of who they are, while remaining faithful to God, the Creator of all things and sustainer of all things.

APPENDIX 1

THE FLOW OF DESTRUCTION OF THE ABORIGINAL PEOPLE

*created by Parry P. Stelter

next page ▶

The Flow of Destruction

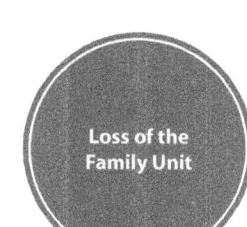

OF THE ABORIGINAL PEOPLE

- Loss of Self-Worth and Language
- The Aboriginal people of North America are victims of a cultural genocide that has had cyclical generational consequences
- Loss of Lands and Hunting
- Vicious Cycle of Abuses of all kinds
- High Suicide and Addictions
- High Incarceration & Unemployment

APPENDIX 2

Definitions

The following definitions in bold font are condensed definitions defined by the Merriam-Webster Online Dictionary. Other definitions in regular font are definitions that I (Parry Stelter) have defined according to my objective research and personal subjective knowledge of the terms and the way in which I chose to use them for this paper. My definitions are not absolute or error free.

Aboriginal: Being the first earliest known of its kind present in a region.

Ancestor: One from whom a person is descended and who is usually more remote in the line of descent than a grandparent.

Animal Spirits: The spirit of an animal that a believer in animism would contact to assist them in their communication with God (The Creator) and the spirit world. The animal spirit varies depending on the culture of the person.

Animism: A doctrine that the vital principal of organic development is immaterial spirit, attribution of conscious life to objects in and phenomena of nature or to inanimate objects; belief in the existence of spirits separable from bodies.

Assimilation: To take in and utilize as nourishment, absorb into the system, to take into the mind and thoroughly comprehend to make similar, to alter by assimilation, to absorb into the culture or mores of a population or group.

Ceremonies: A formal act or series of acts prescribed by ritual, protocol, or convention; a conventional act of politeness or etiquette.

Colonialism: The quality or state of being colonial; something characteristic of a colony; control by one power over a dependent area or people; a policy advocating or based on such control.

First Nation: A recent term that is used to describe the place of land ownership and residence that used to be called "Indian Reservation" or "Reserve." The locations that are called First Nations are places where there have been treaty agreements between the Aboriginal community and the government. The term First Nations is used to improve the reference of the Aboriginal People as being here first. "It is their nation."

Genocide: The deliberate and systematic destruction of a racial, political, or cultural group.

Indian Act: A piece of government legislation that showed how the Aboriginal People of Canada would be governed and provided for in lieu for the lands that the Aboriginal People sold to the government. The land was sold under coercion, rather than through a true and honest business deal.

Indigenous: Produced, growing, living, or occurring naturally in a particular region or environment; innate, inborn.

Mediator: One that mediates between the human race and God. Jesus Christ is referred to as the Mediator between humankind and God. The believer in animism uses animal spirits as a mediator between them and God or the spirit world.

Medicine: A term used by believers in Aboriginal Spirituality that refers to the remedies that a medicine man or medicine woman may use to help a person in their dilemma. There is good medicine and bad medicine. This may take the form of a herb, plant substance, or part of an animal.

Medicine Man/Woman: A person who uses animistic beliefs as a source of power for either good or evil. This person is usually highly respected in the Aboriginal community. They offer help with a variety of issues of life. Whether it be trouble with the law, sickness, or any type of wisdom that is needed. They are usually the one who leads in any given animistic ceremonies such as sweat-lodges, feasts, or sun dances.

Pipe: An object used in smoking tobacco. A handmade object that is used in Aboriginal ceremonies for accessing favor in the spirit world. Using a pipe is part of using proper protocol within many ceremonies. An object used by a medicine man/woman. An object that has to be earned and not bought.

Pow-wow: A festive celebration of dance and song. The dancers wear traditional garments made by hand. Animal spirits are often seen on their garments. The garments are made of items such as leather, sinew, beads, feathers, bells, ribbons, shawls, etc. The dances are for the purpose of accessing the spirit world that includes dead ancestors and animal spirits, and appeasing (Creator) God. There are certain protocols and etiquettes for everyone who is involved. The drummers know the words of the songs and drum beats off by heart. The dancer must keep in tune with the beat of the drummer in order to gain points, which are given out by judges. Some pow-wows are very traditional and some are recreational, where prizes of cash are given out. There are usually several drum groups and the dancers dance around in a circle to the beat of the drum. The more the dancers' footwork lines up with the beat of the drum, the better the dancer they are seen to be. There are several drummers in one drum group. Several drum groups may be asked to drum, just as there are several different kinds of dancers.

Rattle: A device used in Aboriginal Spirituality ceremonies, in the same way a pipe is used: to appease the spirit world and find favor. A devise used by shaking it in one hand and therefore making the noise of a rattle and appeasing the spirits.

Sacred: Dedicated or set apart for the service or worship of a deity, a tree sacred to the gods, devoted exclusively to one service or use worthy of religious veneration. Holy; entitled to reverence and respect of or relating to religion; not secular or profane.

Sage: A plant that is used when communicating with dead ancestors and appeasing the spirit world. The sage is lit on fire by a match and the smoke coming from the sage acts as a mediator to take your prayers to the Creator (God). Believers in Aboriginal Spirituality smudge themselves with the smoke to purify themselves and make themselves clean before the spirit world and the Creator (God).

Salvation: Salvation is a term that refers to the free gift that Jesus Christ gives all people when they believe in Him as Lord and Saviour. They are saved from the works of darkness and Satan. The salvation of a believer is based in the work of Jesus Christ.

Savage: Not domesticated or under human control; untamed; lacking the restraints normal to civilized human beings; fierce; ferocious; wild; uncultivated; boorish; rude; malicious; lacking complex or advanced culture.

Smudging: Smudging is when you take the smoke of a burned substance such as sweet-grass, sage, or tobacco and cover your body with the smoke of that substance. This is done to protect you and purify you from bad spirits and is part of proper protocol in Aboriginal Spirituality ceremonies. It is also to gain favor with the Creator (God) or the spirit world.

Spirit World: The invisible place where the spirits of dead ancestors and animal spirits live. This is the centre of life for the believer in Aboriginal Spirituality.

Spirits: The spirit of a person or animal lives on in the spirit world after death, and these are called spirits. There are also good and bad spirits.

Sundance: A ceremony that is part of the healing process of the Aboriginal People, where they ask for blessing on the future. The sweat-lodge ceremony is usually a part of this ceremony. Prayer and fasting also take place within this ceremony. Usually there is a teepee that is used as the main location for this ceremony. Some tribes have incorporated the piercing of the skin, but not all tribes adhere to this.

Sweat-lodge: This is a place where Aboriginal Spirituality ceremonies take place. The sweat-lodge is made in the form of a circle with certain dimensions in place. They are often made of willow branches and covered with blankets and/or tarps. There is a hole in the middle of the circle for heated rocks to be placed. A medicine man or woman often leads the sweat-lodge ceremonies, but not always. Large rocks are heated in a fire until they turn white; they are then taken out with a pitch fork, so as not to take any ashes with them, as they are placed in the hole in the middle of the circle. There is proper protocol and etiquette when building a sweat-lodge and attending a sweat-lodge ceremony. The sole purpose is to communicate with dead ancestors and the spirit world and seek advice and wisdom in life, which pertain to a variety of issues. The door to the sweat-lodge is closed and in complete darkness when the person in charge of the sweat-lodge ceremony places water on the rocks with something similar to a hyssop branch, causing moisture to heat up the sweat-lodge. The ceremony is often done in what they call rounds. Usually the participants wear bathing suits. Occasionally and rarely people have participated in the nude.

Sweet-grass: Sweet-grass is a grass that is picked and dried and then used as a device to purify and protect yourself with. You take the dried and braided sweet-grass and light it with a match and smudge yourself with the smoke of the sweet-grass. People who believe in Aboriginal Spirituality often hang a braid of sweet-grass in the vehicle or at home for purification and protection from the bad spirits.

APPENDIX 3

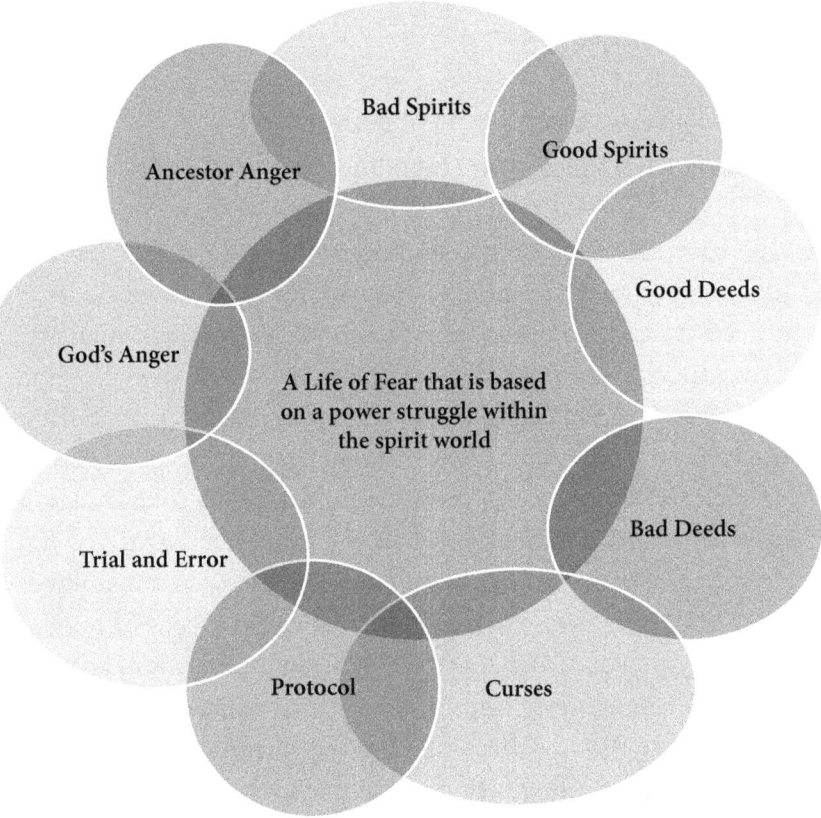

ANIMISM IS BASED ON FEAR

*created by Parry P. Stelter

APPENDIX 4

THE IMPORTANCE OF THE NUMBER 4 IN ABORIGINAL SPIRITUALITY

The spiritual world of the traditional Aboriginal Peoples was designed around the number four, which represented the four directions and the developing and functional aspects of all processes in the universe. Following the design of the medicine wheel, each of the four directions also signified a characteristic such as connectiveness, power (innocence), introspection and models (wisdom). Each direction also featured a color, a season, a creature and an element such as the sun, earth, night and fire. It was contended by the Sioux, for example, that the number four is a cosmic reality. There are four faces or ages of human beings (the face of the child, the adolescent, the adult, and the aged). There are four kinds of things that breathe – those that crawl, those that fly, those that are two-legged, and those that are four-legged. There are four things above the earth – sun, moon, stars and planets – and there are four parts to green things – roots, stem, leaves, and fruit (Friesen, 1995a:119).[62]

ENDNOTES

1 Aboriginal Affairs and Northern Development Canada, n.p. Accessed on June 24, 2011. Online: http://www.ainc-inac.gc.ca/ap/index-eng.asp, n.p.

2 Ibid.

3 John W. Friesen, *Aboriginal Spirituality and Biblical Theology: Closer Than You Think*. Alberta: Detselig, 2000, p 53.

4 Merriam-Webster Dictionary, Cited 9 May 2011, Online: http://www.MerriamwebsterCom/dictionary/, n.p.

5 Raymond Joseph, Armand Huel, *Proclaiming the Gospel to the Indians and the Métis*. Alberta: University of Alberta Press, 1996, p. 144.

6 Nadia, McLaren, "Muffins for Granny," Film Accessed April 29, 2011, Online: http://ca.movienetflix.comWiPlayer?movieid=70144537&trkid=2429428&t=Muffins+for+Granny. 2007, n.p.

7 Nadia McLaren, "Muffins for Granny," n.p.

8 Robin Davey and Yellow Thunder Woman, "Canary Effect," Film, Cited 26 June 2011, 2006, Online: http://www.topdocumentaryfilms.com/canary-effect/ n.p.

9 Robin Davey and Yellow Thunder Woman, "Canary Effect," n.p.

10 Nadia McLaren, "Muffins for Granny," n.p.

11 See Appendix 2 for a outline of the flow of destruction of the Aboriginal Peoples.

12 Dean Halverson (ed.), *The Compact Guide to World Religions: Understanding and Reaching Followers of Islam, Buddhism, Hinduism, Taoism, Judaism, Secularirism, The New Age, And Other World Faiths.* Minnesota: Bethany, 1996, p 25-26.

13 Randal, Rauser, *You're Not As Crazy As I Think: Dialogue in a World of Loud Voices and Hardened Opinions.* Colorado Springs, 2011, p.96,97.

14 Don Richardson, *Eternity In Their Hearts.* California: Regal Books, 1981, p. 131,132.

15 See Appendix 4 for more information on the significance of the number 4 in Aboriginal Spirituality.

16 Worldview Resource Group, *Worldview and Animism*: DVD Set, Disk 2: A Deeper Look: Animistic Worldview, 2010, n.p.

17 Sydney H.T. Page, *Powers of Evil: A Biblical Study of Satan and Demons.* Michigan: Baker, 1995. P. 88,99.

18 See Appendix 3 for more insight

19 Denise Hodgman, *"The Flaw of the Excluded Middle" Among the Cree People of Canada.* Abridged Thesis. n.p. Cited 25 April 2010. Online: http://

www.wrg3.org/21/resources/The%20Middle%20Zone%20Among%20the%20 Cree%20of%20Canada.pdf

20 Mary Dean Atwood, *Spirit Healing: Native American Magic and Medicine*. New York: Sterling Publishing Inc, 1991, p. 70-71.

21 Winfried Corduan, *Neighbouring Faiths: A Christian Introduction to World Religions*. Illinois: InterVarsity Press, 1998, p. 167.

22 Corduan, Ibid., p. 167.

23 Barney, Lacendre, *The Bushman and the Spirits: Spiritual Warfare on the Canadian Frontier*. Saskatchewan: Northern Canada Mission Distributors, 1999, p.151,152.

24 Mary Pat Fisher and Lea W. Bailey (eds.) 2008. *An Anthropology of Living Religions*. Upper Saddle River: Prentice Hall Inc, p. 50.

25 Marie, Burke, Ibid.

26 Ibid.

27 Mary Pat Fisher, *Living Religions* (4th ed). Upper Saddle River: Prentice Hall Inc, 1999, p. 72-73.

28 Christopher, Partridge, *Introduction to World Religions*. Minneapolis: Fortress Press, 2005, p. 120.

29 The Pow-wow is started with a prayer and then the Grand Entry. The Grand Entry is what signifies the beginning of the Pow-wow ceremony, and is where all the dancers and attending Elders come into the circle, as a group, to officially start the ceremony (dancing).

30 Kay Johnston and Gloria Nahanee, *Spirit of Pow-wow*. British Columbia: Hancock House Publishers Ltd, 2003, p. 28-34.

31 David J. Wishart (ed). *Encyclopaedia of the Great Plains Indians*. Nebraska: University of Nebraska-Lincoln, 2007, p.199.

32 David J. Wishart, Ibid.

33 Paul Hiebert, *Understanding Folk Religion: A Christian Response to Popular Beliefs and Practices*. Michigan: Baker Books, 1999, p.168.

34 Daniel R. Shaw, "Contextualizing the Power and the Glory." *International Journal of Frontier Missions*, Vol 12:3 Jul-Sep.1995, n.p. Cited 21 June 2011. Online: http"//www.ijfm .org/PDFs_ IJFM /12_3_ PDFs/08_Shaw.pdf, p. 155,56.

35 Peter S. J. Schineller, "Inculturation and Syncretism: What Is the Real Issue?" *International Bulletin of Missionary Research*, Issue 16:2. April 1992. Cited June 21, 2011. Online: http://www.Internationalbulletin.org/archive/all/1992/4, p.50.

36 Bill Jackson, *Scripture and Traditional Religion*. Saskatchewan: Northern Canada Mission Distributors, 2007, p.17.

37 Jackson, Ibid., p.19

38 Richard, Twiss, "Making Jesus Known: In Knowable Ways." *Mission Frontiers: The Bulletin of the U.S. Center for World Mission*. September-October (2010), p. 9.

39 Paul, Hiebert, "Critical Contextualization." *International Bulletin of Missionary Research*, July 1987, p. 109-110.

40 Victoria Freeman, Distant Relations: *How My Ancestors Colonized North America*. Ontario: McClelland and Stewart Ltd, 2000, p.426.

41 Craig Stephen Smith, *Whiteman's Gospel*. Manitoba: Indian Life Books, 2010, p.80.

42 Craig Ott, Stephen J. Strauss, Timothy C. Tennent, *Encountering Theology of Mission: Biblical Foundations, Historical Developments, and Contemporary Issues*. Michigan: Baker, 2010, p. 275.

43 Terry Muck and Frances S. Adeney, *Christianity Encountering World Religions: The Practice of Mission in the Twenty-first Century*. Michigan: Baker, 2009, p.262.

44 J. I. Packer, *Growing in Christ*. Wheaton, Ill.: Crossway Books, 1996. p. 16.

45 Walter Elwell (ed.), *Evangelical Dictionary of Theology (2nd ed.)*. Grand Rapids: Baker, 2001, p. 1019.

46 Ibid., 1022.

47 Kenneth Boa and William Kruidenier, "Romans" n.p., *Holman's New Testament Commentary* on CD-ROM. Logos Library System Version 4.0c. 2011.

48 Arnold G. Fruchtenbaum, n,p., *The Messianic Bible Study Collection* on CD-ROM. Logos Library System Version 4.0c. 2011.

49 Ibid.

50 Timothy Tennent, *Theology in the Context of World Christianity: How the Global Church is Influencing the Way We Think About and Discuss Theology*. Grand Rapids: Zondervan, 1997, 265-267.

51 Ibid.

52 Bruce A. Demarest and Richard J. Harpel. "Don Richardson's 'Redemptive Analogies' and the Idea of Revelation." *Bibliotheca Sacra* 146 (1989): 330-334.

53 Don Richardson, 2nd ed., *Eternity In Their Hearts*. Ventura: Regal, 1984) 33.

54 Demarest and Harpel. "*Don Richardson's 'Redemptive Analogies' and the Idea of Revelation*," 330-334.

55 Dan Story, *Defending Your Faith* on CD-ROM. Logos Library System Version 4.0c. 2011.

56 Stanley E. Porter and Anthony R. Cross. *Semper Reformation: Studies in Honour of Clark H. Pinnock* on CD-ROM. Logos Library System Version 4.0c. 2011.

57 Ibid.

58 Dean Johnson, Ivan Wells, Victoria Wells, "Missional Community." NA IITS 5 (2007): 59-88.

59 Lawrence E. Sullivan, *Native Religions and Cultures of North America*. London: Continuum, 2003, p. 201-02.

60 Indian Life Newspaper, *The Council Speaks: Answers to Questions Native North Americans are Asking*. Manitoba: Indian Life Books, 1999, p. 65,66.

61 R. L. Gowan (ed.), *Legends of the Trail: Inspiration from Indian Stories, Proverbs and Psalms*. Colorado: International Bible Society, 1997, p.55-56.

62 John Friesen, *You Can't Get There From Here: The Mystique of North American Plains Indians Culture and Philosophy*. Dubuque, IA: Kendall/Hunt, 1995, p.119.

BIBLIOGRAPHY

Aboriginal Affairs and Northern Development Canada, n.p., Cited 24 June 2011. Online: http://www.ainc-inac.gc.ca/ap/index-eng.asp

Atwood, May Dean. *Spirit Healing: Native American Magic and Medicine.* New York: Sterling Publishing Inc., 1991.

Boa, Kenneth, and William Kruidenier. "Romans" n.p., *Holman's New Testament Commentary* on CD-ROM. Logos Library System Version 4.0c. 2011. Printed ed.: Kenneth Boa and William Kruidenier, ed. *Holman's New Testament Commentary.* Nashville: Broadman and Holman Publishing, 2000.

Burke, Marie. "Spirit Doctors" DVD. Canada: National Film Board of Canada, 2005.

Church, Casey. "The Journey of "Hole in the Clouds." *Mission Frontiers. The Bulletin of the U.S. Center for World Mission.* September-October (2010): 15-16.

Corduan, Winfried. *Neighbouring Faiths: A Christian Introduction to World Religions.* Illinois: InterVarsity Press, 1998.

Davey, Robert and Yellow Thunder Woman. "Canary Effect." Film. Cited 26 June 2011, 2006. Online: http://www.topdocumentaryfilms.com/canary-effect/

Demarest, Bruce A., and Richard J. Harpel. "Don Richardson's 'Redemptive analogies' and the Idea of Revelation." *Bibliotheca Sacra*, 146, 1989.

Elwell, Walter, ed. *Evangelical Dictionary of Theology (2nd Ed.)*. Grand Rapids: Baker, 2001.

Fisher, Mary Pat. *Living Religions (4th Ed.)*. Upper Saddle River: Prentice Hall Inc., 1999.

_____, and Lea W. Bailey, eds. 2008. *An Anthropology of Living Religions*. Upper Saddle River: Prentice Hall Inc.

Freeman, Victoria. *Distant Relations: How My Ancestors Colonized North America*. Ontario: McClelland and Stewart Ltd., 2000.

Friesen, John W. *Aboriginal Spirituality and Biblical Theology: Closer Than You Think*. Alberta: Detselig, 2000.

_____. *You Can't Get There From Here: The Mystique of North American Plains Indians Culture and Philosophy*. Dubuque, IA: Kendall/Hunt, 1995.

Fruchtenbaum, Arnold G. n.p., *The Messianic Bible Study Collection* on CD-ROM. Logos Library System Version 4.0c. 2011. Printed ed. *The Messianic Bible Study Collection*.

Halversen, Dean. ed. *The Compact Guide to World Religions: Understanding and Reaching Followers of Islam, Buddhism, Hinduism, Taoism, Judaism, Secularism, The New Age, and Other World Faiths*. Minnesota: Bethany, 1996.

Hiebert, Paul. "Critical Contextualization." *International Bulletin of Missionary Research*. July 1987.

_____. *Understanding Folk Religion: A Christian Response to Popular Beliefs and Practices*. Michigan: Baker Books, 1999.

Huel, Raymond Joseph Armand. *Proclaiming the Gospel to the Indians and the Métis*. Alberta: University of Alberta Press, 1996.

Hodgman, Denise. *"The Flaw of the Excluded Middle" Among the Cree People of Canada*. Abridged Thesis. n.p. Cited 25 April 2010. Online: http://www.wrg3.org/21/resources/The%20Middle%20Zone%20Among%20the%20Cree%20of%20Canada.pdf

Holmes, Arthur and George McPeek. *The Grieving Indian: An Ojibwe Elder Shares His Discovery of Help and Hope*. Manitoba: Indian Life Books, 1988.

Indian Life Newspaper. *The Council Speaks: Answers to Questions Native North Americans are Asking*. Manitoba: Indian Life Books, 1999.

International Bulletin of Missionary Research. "Syncretism: Good? Bad? Inevitable?" Issue 16:2. April 1992. Cited June 21, 2011. Online: http://www.internationalbulletin.org/archive/all/1992/4.

Jackson, Bill. *Scripture and Traditional Religion*. Saskatchewan: Northern Canada Mission Distributors, 2007.

Dean Johnson, Ivan Wells, Victoria Wells. "Missional Community." North American Indigenous Institute Theological Studies 5 (2007): 59-88.

Johnston, Kay and Gloria Nahanee. *Spirit of Pow-wow*. British Columbia: Hancock House Publishers Ltd., 2003.

Lacendre, Barney. *The Bushman and the Spirits: Spiritual Warfare on the Canadian Frontier*. Saskatchewan: Northern Canada Mission Distributors, 1999.

Merriam-Webster Dictionary. Cited 9 May 2011. Online: http://www.MerriamwebsterCom /dictionary/

McLaren, Nadia. "Muffins for Granny." Film. n.p. Cited 29 April 2011. Online: http://ca.movies.netflix.comWiPlayer?movieid=70144537&trkid=2429428&t=Muffins+for+Granny. 2007

Muck, Terry and Frances S. Adeney. *Christianity Encountering World Religions: The Practice of Mission in the Twenty-first Century.* Michigan: Baker, 2009.

Packer, J.I. *Growing in Christ.* Wheaton, Ill.: Crossway Books, 1996.

Page, Sydney H.T. *Powers of Evil: A Biblical Study of Satan and Demons.* Michigan: Baker, 1995.

Partridge, Christopher. *Introduction to World Religions.* Minneapolis: Fortress Press, 2005.

Porter, Stanley E., and Anthony R. Cross. *Semper Reformation: Studies in Honour of Clark H. Pinnock* on CD-ROM. Logos Library System Version 4.0c. 2011. Printed ed. Stanley E. Porter and Anthony Cross. *Semper Reformation: Studies in Honour of Clark H. Pinnock.* Keynes: Paternoster, 2003.

Ott, Craig and Stephen J. Strauss and Timothy C. Tennent. *Encountering Theology of Mission: Biblical Foundations, Historical Developments, and Contemporary Issues.* Michigan: Baker, 2010.

Ramsey, Patrick D. "Judging According to the Bible." *The Journal of Biblical Counselling.* Fall (2002): 62-69.

Rauser, Randal. *You're Not As Crazy As I Think: Dialogue in a World of Loud Voices and Hardened Opinions.* Colorado Springs, 2011.

Richardson, Don. *Eternity In Their Hearts.* California: Regal Books, 1981.

Schineller, Peter, S.J. "Inculturation and Syncretism: What Is the Real Issue?" *International Bulletin of Missionary Research.* Issue 16:2. April 1992. Cited June 21, 2011. Online: http://www.internationalbulletin.org/archive/all/1992/4.

Shaw, Daniel R. "Contextualizing the Power and the Glory." *International Journal of Frontier Missions.* Vol 12:3 Jul-Sep.1995. n.p. Cited 21 June 2011. Online: http"//www.ijfm.org/PDFs_IJFM/12_3_PDFs/08_Shaw.pdf.

Smith, Craig Stephen. *Whiteman's Gospel.* Manitoba: Indian Life Books, 2010.

Story, Dan. *Defending Your Faith* on CD-ROM. Logos Library System Version 4.0c. 2011. Printed ed.: *Defending Your Faith.* Grand Rapids: Kregel Publications, 1997.

Sullivan, Lawrence E. *Native Religions and Cultures of North America.* London: Continuum, 2003.

Tennent, Timothy. *Theology in the Context of World Christianity: How the Global Church is Influencing the Way We Think About and Discuss Theology.* Grand Rapids: Zondervan, 1997.

Twiss, Richard. "Making Jesus Known: In Knowable Ways." *Mission Frontiers. The Bulletin of the U.S. Center for World Mission.* September-October (2010): 6-9.

Wishart, David J. (Ed). *Encyclopaedia of the Great Plains Indians.* Nebraska: University of Nebraska-Lincoln, 2007.

Worldview Resource Group. *Worldview and Animism*: DVD Set, Disk 1-8: A Deeper Look: Animistic Worldview, 2010.

www.ingramcontent.com/pod-product-compliance
Lightning Source LLC
Chambersburg PA
CBHW071728090426
42738CB00011B/2420